"'Legacy isn't what we leave behind, but what we set in motion.' In a me-centered culture, where faith and family take a back seat to financial success and notoriety, this provocative idea changes everything. If you're interested in passing down more than money, not just for your kids but for generations to come, this is the book for you. The powerful, true stories will inspire and empower you to identify and exemplify your mission and values. It's never too late to play your part in God's redemptive story!"

Jim Daly, president, Focus on the Family

"In a world focused on short-term success, my friends David Green and Bill High call us to point our lives heavenward to set in motion a legacy of eternal significance. Like the ripples that emanate from a rock thrown into a pond, our influence for Christ can keep going on and on through our testimony, commitment, and passion for the gospel."

Dr. Robert Jeffress, pastor, First Baptist Dallas;
Bible teacher, Pathway to Victory

"*The Legacy Life* is a practical guide to generational influence. Drawing from his personal journey from humble beginnings, David Green shares how a small loan combined with the legacy of faith he inherited from his parents grew into the founding of Hobby Lobby, which supports countless charities and outreaches. Legacy is far more than money; legacy is a mindset that multiplies. Wherever life finds you, this heartwarming story of the power of belief and family will inspire you."

Lisa Bevere, New York Times bestselling author;
cofounder, Messenger International

"The most exciting adventure that is built into our DNA is to discover the purpose that God has deposited in each one of us. I believe that every human being wants to live a life that matters, but our world offers temporary solutions to silence our God-given ache. I used to try to quiet that cry I felt inside, but now I embrace it as sacred space, a place and a calling that only God can fill. You, too, can live a legacy life. You were made for more."

Sheila Walsh, author and TV host

"*The Legacy Life* is an inspiring call to live with eternity in mind, reminding us that our greatest impact isn't measured in years but in generations. With deep biblical wisdom and practical guidance, this book challenges us to steward our time, talents, and treasures for God's glory and the good of those who come after us. If you're looking to build a life that truly matters, this book is a must-read."

Jordan Raynor, bestselling author, *The Sacredness of Secular Work* and *Redeeming Your Time*

"*The Legacy Life* is a rallying cry to leaders at any age and any level to make a difference, create an impact, leave a mark, and change the world. This book will wake you up to understand the power of multigenerational impact. David and Bill are inviting all of us as leaders to stretch and expand our view of stewardship that will ripple for hundreds of years."
     Brad Lomenick, author, *H3 Leadership* and *The Catalyst Leader*; former president, Catalyst

"David is one of the most intentionally generous and purposeful people I know, making him the best person to write *The Legacy Life*. He absolutely sets the gold standard for investing in a legacy that will not only long outlive him but will have deep and abiding impact for countless generations to come. *The Legacy Life* is an inspiring guide for those seeking to live purposefully in a way that honors God. Drawing from a wealth of personal experience and biblical wisdom, David and Bill challenge readers to shift their focus from temporary success to eternal significance. Their stories and insights encourage us to steward our resources, relationships, and influence with an open hand to serve and give to others, thus reflecting God's heart of generosity. This is a must-read for every follower of Jesus Christ."
     Tom Mullins, founding pastor, Christ Fellowship Church

"Packed with timeless wisdom and real-life application, my friends David Green and Bill High's latest book is a master class on the power of legacy."
     Steve Robinson, pastor, Church of the King, Mandeville, Louisiana

"*The Legacy Life* is an inspiring and practical guide for your personal journey that empowers you to leave a lasting, tangible asset for future generations."
     Ken Polk, CEO and founder, Arlington Family Offices

"I've worked firsthand with business stewards who showcase the impact of intentional legacy-building utilizing the approaches outlined in this well-crafted book. David and Bill approach legacy proactively as the initiatives we set in motion during our lifetime, not what we leave behind. This must-read offers a straightforward guide to legacy perspectives, practices, and adventures. If you're ready to embark on a journey of purpose and impact, look no further than *The Legacy Life*."
     Gayle Kelly, Marketplace Ministry Leader

The
LEGACY
Life

LEADING YOUR FAMILY TO MAKE A
DIFFERENCE FOR ETERNITY

DAVID GREEN
with Bill High

BakerBooks
a division of Baker Publishing Group
Grand Rapids, Michigan

© 2025 by Hobby Lobby Stores, Inc., and Generational Legacy Counsel, LLC

Published by Baker Books
a division of Baker Publishing Group
Grand Rapids, Michigan
BakerBooks.com

Printed in the United States of America

All rights reserved. No part of this publication may be reproduced, stored in a retrieval system, or transmitted in any form or by any means—for example, electronic, photocopy, recording—without the prior written permission of the publisher. The only exception is brief quotations in printed reviews.

Library of Congress Cataloging-in-Publication Data
Names: Green, David, 1941 November 13– author | High, Bill, author
Title: The legacy life : leading your family to make a difference for eternity / David Green with Bill High.
Description: Grand Rapids, Michigan : Baker Books, a division of Baker Publishing Group, [2025]
Identifiers: LCCN 2025002669 | ISBN 9781540904805 (cloth) | ISBN 9781493451111 (ebook)
Subjects: LCSH: Families—Religious aspects—Christianity | Households—Religious aspects—Christianity | Families—Religious life
Classification: LCC BT707.7 .G744 2025 | DDC 248.4—dc23/eng/20250515
LC record available at https://lccn.loc.gov/2025002669

Unless otherwise indicated, Scripture quotations are from the Holy Bible, New International Version®, NIV®. Copyright ©1973, 1978, 1984, 2011 by Biblica, Inc.® Used by permission of Zondervan. All rights reserved worldwide. www.zondervan.com. The "NIV" and "New International Version" are trademarks registered in the United States Patent and Trademark Office by Biblica, Inc.®

Scripture quotations labeled BSB are from the Berean Bible (www.Berean.Bible), Berean Study Bible (BSB). Copyright © 2016–2020 by Bible Hub and Berean Bible. Used by permission. All rights reserved.

Scripture quotations labeled ESV are from the Holy Bible, English Standard Version® (ESV®). Copyright © 2001 by Crossway, a publishing ministry of Good News Publishers. Used by permission. All rights reserved.

Scripture quotations labeled MSG are from *The Message*. Copyright © 1993, 2002, 2018 by Eugene H. Peterson. Used by permission of NavPress. All rights reserved. Represented by Tyndale House Publishers.

Scripture quotations labeled NKJV are from the New King James Version®. Copyright © 1982 by Thomas Nelson. Used by permission. All rights reserved.

Italics added to Scripture quotations reflect the author's emphasis.

Cover design by Chris Gilbert, Studio Gearbox

The proprietors are represented by the literary agency of A Drop of Ink, LLC.

Baker Publishing Group publications use paper produced from sustainable forestry practices and postconsumer waste whenever possible.

25   26   27   28   29   30   31   7   6   5   4   3   2   1

DAVID GREEN

This book is dedicated to the generations that have gone before us—my parents, my grandparents, my great-grandparents, and the generations that I never knew. But it is also dedicated to not only my children and their children, but now my great-grandchildren and the generations yet to come. By faith, I consecrate those generations to come to love God intimately and to live extravagant generosity.

BILL HIGH

I dedicate this book to my wife, my children, and now my grandchildren, who have taught me so much about living the Legacy Life. But I also dedicate this book to all those families who've attended our family legacy workshops, virtually and in person, and the families who have allowed me to work with them in building multigenerational legacies. Without your feedback and willingness to engage, the content in these pages would not be possible.

CONTENTS

Introduction 9

PART 1 LEGACY PERSPECTIVE

1. Searching for Purpose, Searching for Legacy 17
2. Short-Term Thinking: The Enemy of Legacy 29
3. Change Your Lens to a Generational View of Life 43
4. Where Have We Gone Wrong? 57

PART 2 LEGACY PRACTICES

5. Setting Your Course 75
6. Living by a Code of Conduct 89
7. Repairing the Past 103
8. Sharing Your Story 119

PART 3 LEGACY ADVENTURES

9. Thriving Family Legacies of the Bible 137
10. Legacy Families in History 151
11. A Legacy from Brokenness 165
12. Heaven in Sight 179

Closing Thoughts   191
Appendix   195
Acknowledgments   198
Notes   200
About the Authors   208

Introduction

Do you want to live a Legacy Life? A life of meaning and purpose? Do you want to live a life that matters? A life that contributes? A life that counts? A life of significance *for all of eternity*?

I believe that you do. I have yet to meet a person who set out to waste their life. No one sets out on the journey hoping that their life will amount to a meaningless pile of dust and drivel. Truly, in our heart of hearts, we long to live lives of adventure, calling to the deep, innermost parts of our soul.

We are all born with an eternal ache.

We long for something more. We look for meaning. Connection. Belonging. Significance. This ache comes from God.

Is it any wonder that the writer of Ecclesiastes—that book of the Bible that seems to wrestle most with these big questions of life—says, "He has also set eternity in the human heart; yet no one can fathom what God has done from beginning to end" (3:11)?

In this day and age when we measure life by the next text message, the next ding on our phone, we desperately need to rediscover that eternal ache. And not just rediscover it, but seize it, wrestle with it. Otherwise, our life's balance sheet might add up to nothing more than a series of meaningless memes.

What is the secret to the Legacy Life? What is the secret to this life of meaning and purpose? First and foremost, this kind of life is *so much more* than any of us dare dream or imagine. It is so much more than the stuff of this life:

Big bank accounts
Cushy homes
Cool vacations
Sports cars
Fun retirements
The acclaim of many

No, indeed, the Legacy Life is rich and full of virtue. It's a little dangerous. It's a little bold. Because it dares to dream for eternal impact. Yet we must tear ourselves away from our trinkets, our comfort, our screens, and our faint perception. The Legacy Life has impact on the lives of people—our families, our communities, and our world.

For generations.

That's a key missing link. We think far too short-term about our lives. Scripture teaches us that God sees our lives and our families' lives through a generational lens. He sees us having generational impact.

This book is not some kind of self-help book. It's a rallying cry—to see better. To see that our lives are a vapor. We have but one life. We can live a vapor life. Or we can live a life of eternal significance. To live that kind of life, we must see ourselves as stewards. Our God has given each and every one of us a sacred trust. He's placed this one life in our hands and asked us to steward it well.

At the time of this writing, I'm now in my early eighties. As I look at my life, I see more in the rearview mirror than through the windshield. Some might call this the fourth quarter of life. Some might even call it overtime! I say that in jest, but the Scriptures teach us that "the glory of young men is their strength, gray hair the splendor of the old" (Prov. 20:29).

Why do I mention old age? It's not that it gives me superhuman powers, but it does give perspective. The Danish philosopher Søren Kierkegaard is known to have said that life can only be understood backward, but it must be lived forward.

We live in a world of dizzying speed, and the amount of information we take in every single day can be overwhelming. But this information age has tended to bring with it a false pride that we know and see better than previous generations. There's a pendulum effect. We see the mistakes of the previous generations and swing in the opposite direction. As we age, we realize that the shift need not be so dramatic. My appeal is that you would read ahead with a willing heart to explore differently.

So far, I've written three books. The first told the story of Hobby Lobby's founding. The second told our journey of learning to give away 50 percent of our profits and becoming stewards—not owners—of our business. In the third book, *Leadership Not by the Book*, my coauthor Bill High and I recorded the unconventional principles by which I built Hobby Lobby.

One of the chapters from that book was called "Build for 150 Years, Not Just the Next Generation." The sum of that chapter is that we should seek to build not only businesses but families who will thrive for 150 years or more. That chapter captured the attention of many of our readers and became the genesis of this book.

Let me offer a disclaimer. Sometimes one writes as a practiced veteran—much like an accomplished athlete who has practiced a skill over and over. Sometimes one writes looking backward with knowing hindsight. Put more plainly, the one who writes in hindsight says after hard lessons, "I wish someone would have told me to not do that." This book is a mixture of both.

Throughout writing this book, I've also looked to Bill High and his experience consulting hundreds of families on how to live for generational impact. Throughout the book, you'll see some of the practices he's crafted for families and the teachings in his family legacy workshops. The tools have been used by many families, including ours, and we have seen them work.

We've written an accompanying ninety-day devotional called *The Legacy Life Devotional* that we encourage you to read. It gives many of the foundational Scriptures underlying this book.

This book is divided into three sections. The first part focuses on our "Legacy Perspective." We'll redefine what legacy is and stretch your view of your own life and your own family.

In part 2, we'll talk about "Legacy Practices" that give you the opportunity to have the kind of life and family that have an impact for 150 years.

Part 3 is about "Legacy Adventures," where we'll give you real-life stories of success and failure. We'll give you encouragement and hope for your own Legacy Life.

As you read, remember that the Legacy Life applies to you right now.

If you're just starting out, you aren't too young to begin building your Legacy Life. Now is the best time to begin.

If you're nearing your end, even a one-degree change yields big differences in generations to come.

If you're single, your opportunity is no less diminished. Consider Jeremiah, John the Baptist, Paul, and many others.

If you're married, you can work together as a team to accomplish God's vision for your lives.

If you have kids, they contribute to the team effort.

But, even if you don't have kids, legacy doesn't depend on having children.

Your life stage is just that—a stage. Single or married, kids or child-free, young or old—each life situation, when placed in the hand of God, becomes the very tool He uses to craft your unique legacy. For we are *all* His workmanship.

But here's the catch: You cannot live the Legacy Life. That's right—cannot. In your own strength, you will fail. Only God can accomplish this, by His grace. You cannot live the Legacy Life unless your life is pointed toward heaven.

Because legacy is what you set in motion for eternity.

But if we get this right, if our hearts are captured by heaven, we change the world. Imagine generations into the future—thousands of people loving God, all because of a choice you made years ago to be faithful with what God placed in front of you.

So, take heart. Grab hold. And live the adventure of the Legacy Life.

PART 1
LEGACY PERSPECTIVE

1

SEARCHING *for* PURPOSE, SEARCHING *for* LEGACY

> I cry out to God Most High, to God who fulfills his purpose for me.
>
> Psalm 57:2 ESV

Legacy.
  It's just six letters and three syllables. It takes a second to say and a lifetime to live, and its impact is for generations.

But legacy is not what you think it is. When most people think about legacy, they think about dying; "What will you leave behind?" is a popular adage. I think about living. With adventure.

Legacy is like a trip to the mountains or the beach. When you hike in the mountains, it's impossible not to experience some level of humility—to recognize that there are forces greater than you. If you've ever visited the beach, sometimes it's enough to sit and just watch the waves. Timeless. Yet always different. They never stop, and the normal ebb and flow stirs in us a sense of wonder.

> **Legacy is not what we leave behind. Legacy is what we set in motion.**

This is a book about living the Legacy Life, a life of meaning and purpose. But there's a twist. I'd like to change your paradigm. I'm not talking just about your life or the lives of your children or even your grandchildren. I'm talking generations upon generations. Hold that thought for a moment. We're going to get there.

Let's reset the definition of *legacy*. Legacy is not what we leave behind. That's the popular way of thinking about legacy. But to be honest, I think that's too easy. Leaving it behind means that you don't have any responsibility.

I like this definition: *Legacy is what we set in motion.* What will you set in motion for the next 150 years? What will you set in motion for all eternity? What do I mean by "set in motion"?

Set in Motion Your Legacy

Mary was probably just a teenager when her story first unfolded. She lived in a small, nondescript village—Nazareth, population two hundred.[1] The opportunities for upward mobility were small. Most likely, she'd marry a man from her village.

In fact, when the book of Luke opens, she's promised to be married to Joseph. He's a carpenter. But her life changes forever when she's visited by an angel: "Greetings, you who are highly favored! The Lord is with you" (Luke 1:28). She's told that she's going to get pregnant by the Holy Spirit and have a baby. And not just any baby—the Messiah.

On the one hand, it's pretty cool to be visited by an angel. To bear the Messiah would be a big deal too. But there's a problem. Mary is only engaged, and to show up pregnant would be a big problem. She'd dishonor Joseph. She'd dishonor her family. The penalty for an out-of-wedlock birth was death by stoning.

In the moment, her circumstances looked bad. Impossible, even. How was she going to explain this to Joseph? How could she go home and tell her parents she heard from an angel that she was going to have a baby by the Holy Spirit? That just doesn't happen. Who would believe her story? Mary had a different kind of eyesight, however. She had legacy eyesight.

Mary didn't see the moment. She saw far, far ahead. In her Magnificat in Luke 1:46–48, she bursts out:

> My soul glorifies the Lord
>   and my spirit rejoices in God my Savior,
> for he has been mindful
>   of the humble state of his servant.
> From now on *all generations* will call me blessed.

Do you see it? Mary saw a bigger picture. She knew she was setting in motion a powerful legacy. All generations would call her blessed. All generations would be blessed by Mary. All generations would have the opportunity for redemption and restoration.

All because a teen girl from a small town believed, in faith, that God could use her in a grand story. What was Mary's secret for such big eyesight?

Her Magnificat tells us:

> She knew the stories of God's faithfulness to her people in the past (Luke 1:51).
> She knew God had been faithful to her in the past (Luke 1:49).
> She knew God's promise to her people (Luke 1:54–55).

That's one of the first steps in living the Legacy Life: to realize that your life is setting in motion a powerful legacy.

Looking to Generations Past

It would be easy to get caught up in the Hobby Lobby story. Not many businesses start with a $600 loan and grow to have $7.5 billion in sales. Today, we have more than 1,000 stores and 45,000 employees and have been able to give generously to ministries across the world.

But just like Mary, there was a bigger story at work.

My parents, Walter and Marie Green, married in 1933 in Kansas City, Kansas. While I don't know a lot about my dad's family background, I know that my mom's father was an evangelist. In fact, my dad came to Christ at a tent revival led by my mom's father.

They had no big aspirations for business or upward mobility. Instead, they set their hearts on a lifetime of ministry.

The denomination they were in moved them from town to town every two years. It must've been hard packing up and moving so often. Just as you got to know a town and the congregation, it was time to move again. It must've been hard to watch your kids establish friendships only to tell them that it was time to move on again.

They pastored churches over multiple states and multiple cities. The churches they pastored were small—a hundred congregants or fewer. No big crowds. No big offerings. No multisite campuses. I never heard them complain, even though it would have been easy for them to do so. It would have been easy for them to quit under their years of hard labor, but they remained faithful.

My mom died when she was just seventy-one years old. At the time, Hobby Lobby had just opened its second store. She never saw the full bloom. While my dad lived longer, he never saw our maturity either. What kept them going?

> **What kept them going? A simple faith and a belief that they could impact the lives of people for eternity.**

A simple faith and a belief that they could impact the lives of people for eternity. That's it.

Little did they know what they were setting in motion. The faith they planted in me gave wings to something they could never have imagined. Their greatest dream was getting the gospel out to the nations. They never got to see that in a big way.

As Hobby Lobby grew, we committed to what we thought were God-sized giving goals—giving away 50 percent of our profit.

That 50 percent has translated to helping get the gospel out to two billion children around the world through our partnership with One Hope. That 50 percent has translated to thousands of churches planted in some of the most unlikely countries in the world. And that's just the tip of the iceberg of all the things we've been able to do.

All because of two people who lived a simple faith.

Planting Seeds for Generations

Oaks are one of the best trees for building a wooden ship. Of course, it used to be that all ships were made of wood.

The problem with oak trees is that they take a long time to grow.

From 1805 to 1815, Napoleon waged war in Europe.[2] Sweden was one of the countries that opposed him. During the war, Sweden lost more than a hundred ships.[3] Because it was a country vulnerable to attack by way of the Baltic Sea, the replacement of those ships was vital.

By 1830, the Swedish Crown set out to replace those ships and sent out a crew to find ideal spots to plant oak trees for future shipbuilding.[4] One crew came across three beautiful oak trees growing outside an old woman's farmhouse on Visingsö, a small island only accessible by boat.

Knowing that trees suitable for building would take years to mature, the Swedish Navy planted more than 300,000 oak trees over the next ten years.[5] When the trees were first planted, faster-growing trees like ash, elm, and maple were planted between the rows. The oaks were forced to grow straight up toward the light.

Here's the remarkable part of the story. By the time the trees were ready 150 years later (about 1980), shipbuilding had changed. Iron and steel had become the standard.

And Visingsö? There, on nine hundred acres, stood some of the tallest, straightest, and most pristine oak trees. Now that ships are no longer the goal, those oak trees are instead being used for furniture, flooring, and barrels.

The Visingsö forest reminds me of comedian Dennis Swanberg. He tells the story of his great-grandfather Aron Johnson, who moved to West Texas in the 1880s. There, he bought 120 acres, constructed a house, and planted shade trees. Aron and his wife had a son, Carl. But when Carl was just five years old, Aron passed away suddenly.

Swanberg says that his great-grandfather "planted shade trees that he never sat under, but his wife did, and his son did. And my mother did too. And I've had the pleasure of sitting beneath those trees with my two sons. You get the picture: the family has enjoyed those shade trees for over 100 years."[6]

What trees are you planting for generations to come?

Looking to Generations of the Future

When you look at your life through a generational lens, life begins to look different. I've always said that I have one talent and one talent only: to be a merchant. Over the course of running Hobby Lobby for the past fifty years, I've sought to be the very best merchant God would allow me to be.

Yet as I begin to look at my children, I can see a similar generational impact. Let me say that I'm not bragging at all. I'm just learning to look generationally.

My son, Mart, for instance, is now actively engaged in a Bible translation effort called illumiNations. While he's involved in numerous other projects, Bible translation is clearly his number one passion. Today, there are some 7,000 languages in the world. But 3,654—around half—have little or no access to the Bible in their own language.[7]

The idea of completing Bible translation into the last known languages used to be a pipe dream. Not anymore. illumiNations has called together various Bible agencies as well as donors interested in this area to unite to solve the problem.

Think about it—to complete Bible translation in our lifetime. No one could have ever imagined. What kind of impact will that have?

Or consider my son Steve and his wife Jackie. Several years ago, they took on establishing the Museum of the Bible in Washington, DC, as the leaders and drivers behind the project. They've traveled the world, speaking to thousands of people, and they've recruited thousands of donors.

Why? To establish a place where all people can engage with the Bible. Since the doors opened in November 2017, more than three million people have visited the museum.

It is hard to tell all the stories of those who have been impacted by the museum. I'm most encouraged by visitors who come with no faith and lots of skepticism. Yet as they go through the museum, they are invited to consider whether the Bible is true and whether they should at least read it.

Who knows how many millions more the museum might influence from every tribe and nation?

That's just my children. (It's always dangerous to start naming names. All my children, in-laws, grandchildren, and great-grandchildren are absolutely great.) But we already see the same opportunity for generational impact with our grandchildren.

My grandchildren are active in city-reaching movements, education, pro-life advocacy, pastoring, teaching, counseling, the film industry, and many more areas. That's in addition to the important work of raising godly children. And, of course, some of them are continuing leadership inside the company.

Part of what I see in my grandkids that impresses me is their heart for foster care and adoption. They understand God's adoption of us, and they live that out practically in their lives.

The impact doesn't stop there. We are seeing the opportunity with our great-grandchildren too. We hold events for leaders about six to eight times per year. These events are with accomplished leaders who come to hear us share some of our story. My coauthor, Bill, always starts these events by saying that our themes are family, legacy, and generosity.

Just recently, Bill was telling me that we'd be adding a worship component to these events. So not long ago, I walked into one of these events, and there leading worship was my great-granddaughter Mary-Kate. She's just fifteen years old, yet she was leading a room of accomplished leaders in worship.

I don't know where our fourth generation will land. For that matter, our third generation is still carving their path. For both, their greatest accomplishments lie ahead. Of course, it is not all about the accomplishments. I also believe their greatest intimacy with God lies ahead.

Now, I know that some reading these lines will say, "That's fine, David, but my story is not as pretty as yours." All I can say is, don't quit, don't give up, because you don't know what God will do with your faithfulness.

Sometimes You'll Never Know

Perhaps you've heard of the story of Dr. William Leslie. He was born in Ontario, Canada, in 1868.[8] After coming to faith in Christ at age twenty, he began to pursue the idea of going to the mission field.[9] At thirty-five, he set out for the Congo but developed a serious illness. A young nurse named Clara Hill took care of him. Their friendship turned to love, and they married three years later. In 1905, they pioneered a new missions work in Angola, where they suffered through hurricanes, armies of ants, and charging buffaloes.

In 1912, they moved to the Vanga region, located along the Bay of Bengal. With immense effort, they cleared out enough of the jungle to establish a home and a medical outpost. Their hope was that the medical outpost would attract the surrounding tribes, and they could share the gospel. As the Leslies labored away, their best efforts yielded no fruit. Zero. Not one convert.

After seventeen years, a dispute arose, and local tribal leaders finally asked the Leslies to leave. They returned home in 1929, and Dr. Leslie died just nine years later. He considered his life's work a failure.

In 2010, more than eighty years after the Leslies' departure, a missionary team led by Eric Ramsey of Tom Cox World Ministries made a shocking discovery. Upon landing in the Vanga region where the Leslies had been stationed, they found a vibrant, reproducing church.

They visited eight villages with churches—all with their own gospel choir. The local people wrote their own songs and even had gospel sing-offs among the villages. One village's thousand-seat stone cathedral had become so crowded that they needed to engage in a church-planting movement. Thus, the other churches were born.

What happened? How did this evangelistic church-planting effort come about? As Ramsey inquired of these church leaders, they told the story of a man who had come to their villages years before. At least once a year, he traveled through their villages, building an educational system and teaching Bible stories. The tribal people knew he was Baptist but only knew him by one name and couldn't remember if it was his first or last name.

That man was Dr. William Leslie, the man who died thinking he was a failure.

You see, legacy is what we set in motion. Sometimes, we'll never see the fruit of our efforts. But we so often change the trajectories of our legacies with one-degree changes. A little change executed daily leads to an entirely different destination. All it takes is steady obedience in the same direction.

Like Dr. Leslie's work, what seems to be failure may in truth be generational success. We just tend to think too short-term. And that's what we're discussing next.

2

SHORT-TERM THINKING

The Enemy of Legacy

Almost all short-term thinking has long-term pain and short-term relief.

                                          Dave Ramsey

The great enemy of legacy is our short-term thinking. Let me share an early lesson from my own life. When I entered my freshman year of high school, I quickly realized the students lived by a pecking order. The in-crowd versus the out-crowd. At the top stood the athletes and the cheerleaders, then the smart kids, and finally the troublemakers.

I called it the food chain. Everyone envied the kids at the top of the food chain. And then there were the kids like me who didn't even register on the food chain.

As a pastor's kid, I already received a ribbing for my dad's occupation. Even worse, we were poor—not just your average poor, but we were exceptional at being poor.

Now, don't take any of this wrong. I'm not complaining about my childhood. Sorting through secondhand clothes from the missionary bins and running barefoot in the summer was no hardship. I never felt like I was behind or lacking. At least, not until high school.

When I arrived in high school, I discovered the rules of the game had changed. It started to matter what shoes you wore, whether your clothes were in style, and whether you slicked back your hair the right way.

It's possible you could climb up the food chain if you had the right girl on your arm. But I wasn't going to be ready for that for quite some time. If you played sports at an all-conference level, then you could climb up the ladder too. But we had six kids in our family, and we had neither the time nor the money to prefer one kid's sports habit over another. Of course, another option was to have a really cool car, which would really set you apart. But I was out of luck there too—I was only in the ninth grade and driving was still on the horizon.

So, what did I do? I joined the band. I'm not sure what possessed me to think that a class in music would move me up the food chain. In truth, I didn't have much choice. Music was a required course. I couldn't sing, which meant the choir was out. Band it was.

The optimism of joining band was short-lived. I ended up in the clarinet section. I'm not sure what high school bands look like today, but back then the clarinet section was populated solely by girls. My ranking on the food chain was sinking even lower.

It got worse. For those of you who don't know, the clarinet is what they call a woodwind instrument. While I certainly boasted plenty of wind, I lacked a particular skill. Let me explain.

The clarinet has a mouthpiece that has a bamboo reed. To get the proper sound coming out of a clarinet, you must apply the right pressure with your mouth on the reed to make it vibrate correctly. It's not an easy task to get your lips just right on a razor-thin bamboo reed. If you don't get it perfect, then the clarinet squeaks and squawks. Do you see where this is going?

I couldn't just rely on my ample wind. I needed skill to make that clarinet sound rich and mellow. I never did get to mellow, but I was able to make it sound like a flock of ducks trying to avoid a hunter's shotgun. The band director was none too pleased, and I sunk lower still on the chain. I was the last chair clarinet player.

Worse still, when I took a break from playing my duck-call clarinet tunes, I looked up across the room, and there was Frankie Valli. Honestly, I can't remember his real name, but he looked like Frankie Valli, the lead singer of the Four Seasons. (For my grandkids' generation, picture the latest popstar.)

Frankie was cool. His hair was slicked back, neat, and stylish. His clothes were department store fresh, and I'll never forget it as long as I live: His pants were creased. I mean, who does that?

Even better for Frankie, he played the trumpet. I suppose I should say he performed on the trumpet. The band director gave him the solo parts. Frankie smiled, and the girls swooned, including all the cheerleaders.

And I, in my ninth-grade mind, not even ranking on the food chain, began to seriously dislike and envy Frankie—for the slicked-back hair, the in-style clothes, the first chair trumpet solos, and most of all, the creases in his pants.

I should have sensed something was about to go awry. In my youthful energy, I didn't have the benefit of hindsight. I only had the sheer power of the moment.

I smile now when I think of what transpired next. My eighty-year-old self with my well-earned gray hair wants to reach across time and pat my fourteen-year-old self on the head and say wisely, "Now think, David!"

But I didn't. I plunged on ahead. For me, it was all about ready, fire, and aim later. I'd decided to pick a fight with Frankie Valli. Lest you think I'm vain or a bully, it was not so uncommon for kids growing up in the 1950s to end up in scrapes after school. I'd ended up in a few of them in my day. And I have to say that I was a strong, wiry fellow who held up pretty well in those youthful standoffs.

Until Frankie Valli.

Now, all these years later, the details of that tussle are a blur. Maybe my mind chose to forget the details. I just know that I was the one to initiate the skirmish with Frankie. Strong and confident, I called him out.

That confidence was soon buried under a barrage of elbows and fists. I was on the bottom looking up, and Frankie thrashed me pretty good.

I had fallen victim to my own short-term thinking. My energy and my youth did not give me the foresight to realize the battle might not go my way.

Symptoms of Short-Term Thinking

While my Frankie Valli moment is written with humor, it illustrates the trouble of our times. I made a decision on a whim. I gave in to the school's temporary definition of success: social status, fashion, looks, and popularity. And while my temporary skirmish bruised my pride, it left little long-term damage.

Unfortunately, not all short-term decisions have such short-term consequences.

Think about it. We live in a world of short-term behaviors.

- *People are searching.* Literally. There are over 255,600 Google searches per second, and 15,336,021 per minute.[1]
- *We can't put our phones down.* The average person touches their cell phone 2,617 times per day.[2]
- *We can't pay attention.* From 2000 to 2015, the average attention span dropped from 12 seconds to 8.5 seconds. A goldfish has an attention span of 9 seconds.[3]
- *We make a lot of decisions.* The average person makes 35,000 decisions per day, 2,000 decisions per hour, one decision every 2 seconds.[4]
- *It's going faster.* A whopping 74 percent of people say the number of decisions they make has gone up ten times in the last three years.[5]

More decisions. More information. Our world has taught us to think short-term about our personal lives, our careers, our businesses, and our families. We face information overload. We are nearing 180 zettabytes of global data.[6] I don't know what a zettabyte is, but it sure sounds like a lot. Here's the important point: 76 percent of the people in the United States believe that information overload contributes to their daily stress.[7]

What has all this short-term decision-making produced? You'd think that all this digital information and digital connection would produce greater happiness. Instead, the effect has been the opposite. The *AMA Journal of Ethics* said it this way: "An early study of the internet and psychological well-being found that greater internet use was associated with a decline in participants' communication with family members, a decrease in their social circle, and an increase in depression and loneliness."[8]

That's a very long and scientific way of saying that our short-term decision-making is leading us away from what we want most in life.

From meaning.

From connection.

From purpose.

Living for the short term has taken away our sense of hope and purpose. That lost hope is reflected in the rise of social anxiety disorders we see today. Each year in the United States, fifteen million people are diagnosed with social anxiety disorder.[9] The National Institutes of Health have categorized an entirely new class of disease: They call them the diseases of despair, or DoD—alcohol misuse, substance misuse, and suicidal ideation.[10]

As just one example of this pervasive short-term mindset, suicide is the second leading cause of death for those ages ten to thirty-four.[11]

All of these things suggest that we are losing hope in our story. We don't see the bigger picture. We are living and thinking short-term.

Toward a Legacy View

We don't think long-term like we used to. It used to be that our efforts around our lives were collectively built around this idea of stewardship. We were stewards for the next generation and the coming generations. Whether it was the farm or the business, we saw ourselves as making the world a better place for our children and our grandchildren.

We don't think like that anymore. We live in a microwave world, not a Crock-Pot world. Consider the following examples to the contrary.

The oldest continuous operating family business is a hotel in Japan. It was started in AD 718[12] and has been operated continuously by the same family for 1,300 years. Previously, the oldest family business was a construction company in Japan that was started in AD 578. It operated for 1,400 years before selling out to private equity in 2006.[13]

Japan does not stand alone. If you go to Germany, for instance, the top-ten oldest family-owned businesses have been in business for four hundred years each—all dating back to the 1500s.[14] In Italy, the tale is even longer, with fifteen of the world's oldest family-owned businesses. The oldest five date to AD 1000, 1141, 1295, 1369, and 1385.[15]

We could go to virtually every part of the world and find similar stories of families who have persisted together for hundreds of years. In the United States, the oldest family-owned business is Zildjian. It was founded in 1623 in Constantinople but moved to the United States in 1929. Otherwise, the next three oldest all have 150 years or fewer of history.[16]

> **We acted as stewards for the next generation.**

Please don't miss what I'm saying. This is not a book about business. This is a book about your life and your family. The real point of sharing the stories of these long-lasting families is to emphasize the idea that we used to think and plan like that.

We acted as stewards for the next generation.

A Parable of Stewardship

There's a powerful parable I heard years ago. It's the story of a man in Japan who walked to work every day. Each day, he passed by a field where a farmer was clearing rocks from the field. The farmer picked, he dug, and then he carried the rocks to the side of the field. Every day, every season, the routine was the same.

Finally, the man grew curious. Why did the farmer never plant a crop? Why did he only carry rocks to the side of the field?

He stopped the farmer in the midst of his work. He repeated his thoughts: "Every day, I walk to work, and I walk by this field. Every day, I see you do the same thing. You pick, you dig, and you carry rocks to the side of the field. Why do you never plant a crop?"

The farmer smiled patiently and responded, "I'm preparing this field for my grandchildren."

A Biblical Mindset

This principle of stewardship is not a business principle. It's a biblical principle. When you look at the life of Abraham, in Genesis 12, he is promised a land and a people and told he will be a blessing to the world.

But there's one problem. He doesn't have a son, so how can the blessing take place? Abraham waits twenty-five years before he gets a son—to the point that the promise seems unbelievable. Beyond that, Abraham never does get the land.

In fact, God tells him that his descendants will go down to Egypt and be in slavery for four hundred years. Then, after four hundred years, they will come back and take the land. I don't know about you, but I don't think I'd want to wait for four hundred years to occupy the land I'd been promised.

And the last promise to Abraham—to be a blessing to the world? Well, in Matthew 1:17, we are told, "Thus there were fourteen generations in all from Abraham to David, fourteen from David to the exile to Babylon, and fourteen from the exile to the Messiah." If you are doing the math, that's forty-two generations before the promise of the blessing to the world gets fulfilled.

Let's pause for a moment. While we tend to skip the genealogies, the Bible is careful to record them. In fact, if you flip back to Genesis, you'll see a similar precision. In Genesis 5, there are ten generations from Adam to Noah. In Genesis 11, there are another ten generations from Noah to Abraham. In all, there are sixty-two generations from Adam to Christ.

Why are all these generations important? Through this seemingly irrelevant data point around genealogy, God demonstrates the relentless drumbeat of a central theme. Time and time again, over and over, He reminds us: "I am the God of your father, the God of Abraham, the God of Isaac, and the God of Jacob" (Exod. 3:6). He authors only one story, and that story's theme is marked by His great love and mercy toward us. In that one story, He is always pointing us toward restoration and redemption in Christ.

We are just part of that story. We are not our own story. We are part of that one.

In the Lord's careful way, He is reminding us, "Don't think short-term. Think long-term. Think of the long tomorrow." This generational view cuts against how we think of long-term planning in our world today.

Of Retirement and Family

In our Western world, our best long-term thinking tends to be built around the concept of retirement.

As a result, we think of our family as a nest. We keep our children in that nest at least until eighteen years of age. We hover over them and protect them. But once they hit eighteen, we kick them out of that nest and expect them to make their own way in the world. I'll talk more about this in chapter 4, but for now, stick with me in the vein of retirement.

At the empty-nest stage, we tend to see our children as fully independent, free to do whatever they want. Meanwhile, as parents with our initial duties done, the mindset in the empty-nest stage is "me time!" Because we are "done" with our parenting, we can finally retire. Bill calls this the "up and out" theory—raise them up and kick them out so we can retire and play golf. In fact, we can even move away from our children and grandchildren to a warmer climate and spend our days focused on ourselves.

For instance, in my life situation, the normal expectation is that I'd simply retire and move to Florida or someplace that has better weather than the blistering heat, wind, and tornadoes of Oklahoma. I'd probably take up golf or some other kind of hobby. Uh, no thank you. I think I'd rather become a greeter at a Hobby Lobby!

This idea of retiring and traveling or even moving somewhere fun has only popped up during my lifetime. During my parents' lifetime, the majority of Americans lived and worked until they died. There was no such thing as slowing down. As the concept of retirement became popular, retirement communities began to spring up.

Del Webb, head of a construction company, invented a retirement community in Arizona called Sun City. Only people aged fifty and up could buy homes. No kids allowed. Elderly people left their families and bought homes by the hundreds. Webb filled Sun City with activities—golf, pottery, painting, bicycling, bocce ball. But no kids.

In 1962, *Time* magazine featured Webb as their man of the year—all because he got an entire generation of people to focus on themselves. I'm not trying to say retirement is all bad, but what happens when we begin to move grandparents away from the family? This retirement syndrome reflects the highly individualistic, self-centered world we live in.

As a reflection of this move away from family to the focus on individuals, take a look at these statistics: In 1960, the majority of kids—73 percent—were growing up in homes with two parents who were both in their first marriage.[17] By 2014, that number had dropped to 46 percent.

In *Don't Waste Your Life*, John Piper writes of a couple who retired early in their fifties, bought a boat, and traveled the coast of Florida playing softball and collecting shells. Piper writes, "Tragically, this was the dream: come to the end of your life . . . and let the last great work of your life, before you give an account to your Creator, be this: playing softball and collecting shells. Picture them before Christ at the day of judgment: 'Look, Lord. See my shells.' *That* is a tragedy."[18]

> **We need a call to a Legacy Life mindset—a long-term mindset.**

I pray that we will be called out of this retirement thinking and into a mindset that a battle still rages for the hearts and souls of people around the globe. As long as there are people who don't know Jesus, we are called to keep working for the advancement of the gospel.

We need a call to a Legacy Life mindset—a long-term mindset.

A Call to Long-Term Thinking

Even now, I think about my Frankie Valli moment. And I realize the brashness of my teen years continued into my twenties. While some of that growth was healthy, I know that my parents had to cringe at times, as they saw me be so full of myself.

When I got my first promotion at work, I was bursting with pride. I immediately came home and told my mom. She responded, "Well, David, what are you doing for the Lord?"

When I got my second big promotion, her response was exactly the same: "Well, David, what are you doing for the Lord?"

I've sometimes joked that even if I came home and said, "Mom, I was just voted the president of the United States," she'd still have the same response.

Now, some of you might cringe at my mom's response. In fact, you might say, "Shame on her!" In today's society, we'd want to correct her and tell her that kids need affirmation and praise. I'm afraid our society is filled with too many certificates for participation.

In the eyes of the world, my mom's balance sheet looked bare. She died with a handful of clothes and not enough in her bank account to pay for her funeral. I paid for her funeral. But in the eyes of heaven, her bank account was overflowing with a heart that loved God until the end, faithful service to the church, a marriage that lasted until death, and six children who served the Lord. She was so wealthy that God sent His angels to take her home on her deathbed.

Moments before she passed away, she sat up in bed and exclaimed to my sister, "Do you see them? Do you see them?" And then she lay down and breathed her last. We can only guess what she saw, but we imagine it was a company of angels sent to take her home.

I thank God for my mom. And oh, I wish there were more Marie Greens in this world today. We need people like her who would remind us that the promotions and trappings of this world mean nothing. How we need to ask our stony hearts that question again and again to shake us out of the reverie of the temporary moments of this earth:

What are you doing for eternity?

My mom's questions kept pointing me to the long term. She helped me wrestle with my career decisions until I could see clearly how my life and calling impacted the kingdom of God.

As the years have passed, I realize she was calling me to a legacy mindset. The legacy mindset reminds me that I own nothing on this planet. For a brief time, a vapor, God entrusts me with a few things—people, influence, talent, and treasure.

The Lord's challenge to each of us is: How will we steward what He's put in our hands? Stewardship means my resources are not just for me. I'm a steward of the story God started in our family. My job is to make a great handoff to my children, grandchildren, and great-grandchildren. For that generational handoff, my hope and prayer are that He might say, "Well done."

This stewardship mindset—for the generations—begins to change everything.

It moves us from short-term thinking to long-term thinking. We can now dive into the generational mindset.

3

CHANGE YOUR LENS *to a* GENERATIONAL VIEW *of* LIFE

> Time should be measured by the generation.
> James Hughes

If you've learned anything so far, thank Frankie Valli—we think too short-term. But in addition to our short-term thinking, we look at our world through the wrong lens. When I was a kid growing up, we moved from town to town. My parents pastored churches in six states: Arizona, California, Kansas, Oklahoma, New Mexico, and Texas. We lived in eight different cities in those states. I was born in Emporia, Kansas—a small town of ten thousand people.

Every church my parents pastored was small. The biggest church was a hundred people. That's it. Small towns, small schools, small offerings. Many times the offerings didn't come in the form of cash; instead, we got vegetables from a family's garden. Those simple offerings meant simple meals. It was a big day if someone donated a chicken.

I remember that in one of those small towns there was an elderly single woman who showed compassion on our family. She told us that she and her boyfriend wanted to help us out. And boy did they! They gave us *steaks*. Now that was a treat, to put it mildly.

My sister Lois, who was a bit of a busybody, decided that this lady wasn't telling us the truth, and she wanted to ask this woman about her supposed boyfriend. Fearing the loss of those steaks, I told Lois in no uncertain terms, "Lois, just leave it alone! If she wants to give us steaks, let her!"

I digress. My eyesight was pretty limited. I had no view of crowded stadiums, megachurches, and flashing billboards. Our pantry was barely stocked with enough food for the week.

It wasn't until we lived in Altus, Oklahoma, when I was seventeen years old, that my eyesight began to change. I never had much love for school, so I enrolled in Distributive Education, which allowed me to take three classes—Math, English, and Distributive Education—and I got a credit for working. I was out of school most everyday by 10:30 a.m. and off to work at TG&Y, the local five-and-dime.

At that time, I had no dream of Hobby Lobby or anything remotely resembling that. My eyesight was on my next paycheck. But as I worked, I realized that I was good at it. I got appointed to set up the window displays. My displays seemed to catch the attention of customers. My boss, T. Texas Tyler, took a liking to me. That's where the dream first began to form that I could be a store manager.

That was a pretty big dream for me, coming from my background. I'd never seen a big organization. I'd never seen anything grow and scale. On the status scale of life, all I'd ever known was "pastor's kid" and "poor." But, hey, store manager meant a position, a title, a place of authority. It was more than I could conceive of, but it placed a dream inside of me that was far bigger than anything I'd had up to that point in time.

I just needed to change my lens—how I viewed my world.

Understanding How Eyesight Works

I've been wearing glasses now for what seems like most of my life. Without glasses, my eyesight is vague, blurry, even dim. I wouldn't know if the speed limit was 35 mph or 55 mph without my glasses. But when I slip my glasses into place, it's amazing how what was fuzzy becomes sharp and defined.

Eyesight is a wonderful but intricate gift. The eye is the second-most-complex organ in the body, next to the brain. There are over two million parts of the eye. Here's a rough, simplified view of how we get eyesight.

Light first passes through the cornea, which is the clear front layer of the eye, and must ultimately pass through the lens of the eye. The lens bends the light to the back of the eye, which contains photoreceptors. Those receptors turn the light into electrical signals that get transmitted through the optic nerve to the brain. The brain then interprets those images.[1]

Glasses work by bending the light rays differently, which makes those fuzzy images become clear.

All it takes is a simple change of lens.

My problem for most of my early days was that my vision was too short-term. I focused on the immediate—getting through school, reaching summer break, landing my first job, buying my first car, getting married, having kids, establishing a career. There's nothing wrong with these things, but they were too nearsighted.

> **But what if we are thinking far too small? We need to install a God-sized lens.**

When we think of our lives, we tend to think seventy or eighty years. We live, we breathe, we die. We get married, we have kids, and maybe we live to see our grandchildren, if we have good health. Particularly in today's world, as people are getting married later and later, it is rare that we might see our great-grandchildren.

Flip over to the financial planning world. Long-term thinking is the idea of forty years of work and then retirement. The big idea there is compound interest. If you start sowing for retirement at twenty-five years of age, then you'll be ready to retire at sixty-five because of the power of compound interest. These types of plans are praised as the pinnacle of planning ahead. But what if we are thinking far too small?

We need to install a God-sized lens.

Our God looks at our lives through a generational lens.

The Generational Lens of God

As we consider the lens by which we should view our lives, our families, and the world, we should consider the very nature and character of God. He is everlasting. Isaiah 40:28 proclaims, "The LORD is the everlasting God, the Creator of the ends of the earth."

When God speaks to Moses in the wilderness, He introduces Himself as a generational God: "I am the God of your father, the God of Abraham, the God of Isaac and the God of Jacob" (Exod. 3:6). Why is He generational in nature? Because He is a God of order, not of chaos, as Paul tells us (1 Cor. 14:33). In the same way, Isaiah reminds us that when God puts a plan in motion, no one can change it (Isa. 14:27). The psalmist reminds us that the purposes of God's heart extend through all the generations (Ps. 33:11).

God Thinks and Plans Generationally

The implications of the generational character of God start with the fact that He thinks and plans generationally. In the last chapter, we saw that Abraham was given a generational promise. God's plan was to bless the world through Abraham's family. They'd occupy a narrow strip of land called Canaan, but it would take four hundred years before the land could become theirs. Genesis 17:7 is one illustration of the generational nature of God's promise to Abraham: "I will establish my covenant as an everlasting covenant between me and you *and your descendants after you for the generations to come*, to be your God and the God of your descendants after you."

As we follow the succeeding generations, we see God work in the lives of Isaac, Jacob, Judah, Joseph, Moses, Joshua, Samuel, David, Solomon, Rehoboam—well, you get the idea. God put in motion one story. It is one story of redemption and restoration. The entire story points to Christ and His death, burial, and resurrection. Our individual lives are not the story. We are only part of the story.

God's Promises Are Generational

Given the generational nature of God, it is consistent with His character that He makes generational promises. In addition to the generational promise to Abraham, God promised to Noah that there would never be a flood that would destroy the earth (Gen. 9:11). On a grander scale, God promised to David that his house and his kingdom would endure (2 Sam. 7:16). On a smaller scale, God told Jehu that his descendants would rule for four generations after him (2 Kings 10:30).

Perhaps one of the most amazing generational promises is found in Exodus 20. There, in verse 5, God says that He'll punish those who chase after other gods to the third and fourth generation. Okay, that wasn't the amazing part. You've got to look at verse 6. There, God says He'll show love *to a thousand generations* of those who love and keep His commandments!

God Expects Generational Commitment

In keeping with His generational character, God expects a similar behavior from His people. He doesn't want just Abraham to keep His commandments. Or just Moses. Or just Joshua. Or just me. He wants generations of faithfulness.

For instance, the Passover festival was considered a celebration to be carried on through the generations. Exodus 12:14 says, "This is a day you are to commemorate; *for the generations to come* you shall celebrate it as a festival to the LORD—a lasting ordinance." In Leviticus 23, a casual reading of each of the seven festivals tells us they are to be "a lasting ordinance for the generations to come, wherever you live" (v. 14).

Queen Esther's rescue of her people led to the festival of Purim. The command was "that these days should be remembered and kept *throughout every generation*, every family, every province, and every city" (Esther 9:28 NKJV).

Remind the Future Generations

The generational commitment assumes that we will tell the coming generations of God's work in our lives. For instance, in Joel 1:3 we are reminded, "Tell it to your children, and let your children tell it to their children, and their children to the next generation."

As another illustration, the psalmist Asaph says it this way:

> [God] decreed statutes for Jacob
>   and established the law in Israel,
> which he commanded our ancestors
>   to teach *their children*,
> so the next generation would know them,
>   even the children yet to be born,
>   and they in turn would tell their children.
> Then they would put their trust in God
>   and would not forget his deeds
>   but would keep his commands. (Ps. 78:5–7)

Did you catch how many generations are mentioned in those few verses? Five generations! Asaph is wanting the coming generations to know the work that God has done for them. The parables. The stories. Splitting the Red Sea. Gushing water from a rock. Lighting a pillar of fire to guide them. Raining manna when they hungered for bread. Sending quail when they craved meat.

But he also wants them to know God's commands—His instructions on how they should live their lives to honor Him. The Ten Commandments. The law. Moses's pleading from the mountaintop, "This day I call the heavens and the earth as witnesses against you that I have set before you life and death, blessings and curses. Now choose life, so that you and your children may live" (Deut. 30:19). These verses demonstrate the generational handoff that God desires that we follow.

One more additional fact: We know that Asaph was the chief musician in David's court and Solomon's court. But we also know, according to Nehemiah 7:44, that there were 148 sons of Asaph still in pursuit of God—some five hundred years later! Asaph lived out the generational mandate.[2]

A Five-Hundred-Year Lens

Think of the life of Daniel the prophet. We don't know a lot of details of his life. We know that Daniel was a captive. We don't know if he was married or if he had children. When the king of Babylon conquered Jerusalem, he took not only their treasures but also their young men of the royal family and nobility (Dan. 1:3). Daniel is one of those young men. As a captive in the king's court, Daniel might have easily given in to peer pressure. He quickly could have conformed to the ways of the foreign king to increase his standing.

Instead, Daniel chooses to stand out. He refuses to eat the food of the royal court. He opts for a simpler diet of vegetables and water. In the court of Babylon, Daniel becomes known as a man of biblical wisdom. He refuses to side with the magicians and astrologers of the day. In fact, no one can challenge Daniel's conduct—except on the grounds of his faithfulness to pray three times a day. It's his faithfulness to pray only to God that ultimately lands him in the lion's den.

When we look through a traditional lens at Daniel's life, we can easily get lost in his accolades. Our Western world would trumpet Daniel's individual achievements, his wisdom, his faithfulness, and his courage. Daniel stands out with a glowing résumé.

Any one of us would hire Daniel as the next senior vice president or make him the senior pastor of our church.

But if we see only his personal accolades, we miss the larger point of Daniel's life. Certainly, in Daniel's individual life, he stood out as a man who stood against the tides of culture. Yet Daniel also wrote a book. His words and his life and his prophecies would impact future generations of believers.

Still, there's another interesting twist from Daniel's life.

Fast-forward to the Christmas story. In Matthew 2:1–2, the Bible records: "Magi from the east came to Jerusalem and asked, 'Where is the one who has been born king of the Jews? We saw his star when it rose and have come to worship him.'"

These wise men from the east play a crucial role in the Christmas story. They bring gifts of gold, frankincense, and myrrh to Jesus and His family. All of these items hold obvious value, and quite likely these gifts became the means to fund the escape of Jesus, Mary, and Joseph to Egypt.

So where did these wise men come from besides "the east"? Many scholars believe these wise men were Persians who came from Babylon.[3] How did these Persians—these Babylonians—know about a Jewish prophecy and realize that they should look for a King who would shape the course of human history?

While we cannot know Daniel's exact influence for sure, we do know from Daniel 5:11 that he was chief of the magicians. His prophecies became known throughout the Far East. It's quite likely that the Magi of Matthew 2 had studied or been influenced by the writings of Daniel.

And how much time had passed from the writings of Daniel to the arrival of the Magi in Matthew 2?

At least five hundred years.[4]

While there isn't conclusive evidence to link Daniel to the Magi of the Christmas story, it isn't a far stretch to see the connection either. But that's part of the point. Sometimes we don't know what impact we'll have on future generations.

We know that Daniel lived faithfully. He sought to do what God wanted, even in a culture where he stood out like a sore thumb. He wrote down his experiences and chronicled them in a book for the benefit of others. Certainly, he did not have full understanding of this impact. But some five hundred years later, we see the traces of his handiwork. Quite likely, his words impacted a group of wise men, compelling them to leave their home and put their lives in danger—all to visit who they believed to be a child-king.

That's a Legacy Life.

The Power of Generational Influence

The Scriptures teach other stories of generational influence besides Daniel's. You'll find some of those in chapter 9. For now, some of you might be asking the question, "How can I have generational influence? I'm not a Daniel, a scholar in the court of a king!"

Let me take you back to part of my story. As I mentioned earlier, when I was growing up, my parents were part of a denomination that moved their pastors every two years. I sometimes joke that the denomination must have thought that a pastor would run out of sermons every two years, so they had to move on.

Nonetheless, when the time came, we'd pull out the boxes again. Our clothes, our shoes, our meager possessions—such as they were—all packed again. My dad never owned a car, so that meant we'd have to have someone help us move. I remember one old cotton truck that we managed to put a sofa at the front of. All of us kids piled on that sofa, and it was great fun. Until it started raining.

Our homes weren't ones we selected. Instead, it was the next parsonage, often a two-bedroom home, and kids had to sleep in the living room to make it all work. Finances were tight. On the rare occasion when someone donated a chicken for our family dinner, we had to make that chicken stretch to feed eight people. This meant that my dad had to eat the neck of the chicken. And, well, there's not a lot of meat on the neck.

Those vagabond ways do something to you. Our schools were temporary. Our teachers were temporary. Our friends were temporary. Our congregations were temporary. It was as if everyone played the game with us, but everyone knew we'd soon be moving on. I was already pretty shy, so these temporary stops didn't help much. It might have been something that could have created bitterness inside of my young soul.

But no matter how many times my boxes were packed and unpacked, no matter how many dusty towns we rolled into, no matter how small the parsonage, no matter how scant the offerings, our family just kept plugging away.

Let's be honest. It probably would have been easier for my dad to quit the pastoring life and just go get a job. He could have stayed in one place and had an easier time supporting his family. Looking back now, I suspect that it was hard for my parents to watch their children—our family—survive on meager rations. We took government help; those days we called them commodities—things like powdered milk, potato flakes, and canned butter. It was the only way to make things work.

Why struggle like this?

The Call to Faithfulness

Looking back with the benefit of my eighty-plus years and a generational lens, I can see it so much more clearly now. My mom and dad were faithful with what God put in front of them. That's all they wanted: to be faithful with their marriage, their children, their church, the parsonage, the people in their congregations.

I think another part of the message here is that God is okay with us being uncomfortable. It's okay to have some struggle along the way. It's a good thing for us to not see all the way to the end. We remain faithful not knowing what the future holds. That's what faith is.

The beauty of living faithfully right now is that we can trust the results to God. We do not and cannot know what He'll do in future generations. God is in the results business. Our business should be in faithfulness.

As you read these words, I hope that you hear the message here. Be faithful right where you are at. Be faithful with whatever God has put in your hands.

Even if you are an exile away from your home, like Daniel.

Even if you are without a car. Without your own house. With less financial means than you'd like.

Even if it seems like you get moved around by the choosing of others.

Even if you have a lot.

Just be faithful with whatever your circumstances are. My mom stepped into the faith of her dad. I stepped into the faith that I saw in them. My children stepped into the same faith they saw in us. Now there are grandchildren and great-grandchildren living out that same faith. That's six generations.

While we are not at five hundred years yet, my plan is to remain faithful as the first step to that five hundred years. It reminds me of Hebrews 11, the Hall of Fame of faith. There we are reminded of the great struggles of those we might call our heroes with the plain and simple notation: "These were all commended for their faith, yet none of them received what had been promised, since God had planned something better for us so that only together with us would they be made perfect" (vv. 39–40).

Now that we have a generational lens in place, let's ask this question: Where have we gone wrong?

4

WHERE HAVE WE GONE WRONG?

> Time was when the whole of life went forward in the family, in a circle of loved, familiar faces.
>
> Peter Laslett

There should be a glaring question in your mind by now: If God's design for my life and my family is for generational impact, then what happened? Where did we go wrong? How did we end up with such short-term thinking?

I'd call it a failure of family worldview.

Or call it a failure of stewardship. We've been using the wrong lens for family. We've allowed Western culture to define our lives and the family instead of the Bible.

Now, as I write, I recognize that the majority of adults in the US are unmarried. And almost half of adults do not have children. So if you don't have a spouse or kids, don't disregard this chapter. This information still applies. As a culture, we've been led down a wrong road, and getting back on the right path matters. Whether or not you have a spouse, kids, or grandkids, how you view family matters.

In this chapter, I'll share generalities about families. Not all of them apply to every situation. But it is important for every person to know where we've come from and how far we've strayed.

Family Worldview—How It Used to Be

When I was growing up in the 1940s, my family seemed typical of most families.

The dad often worked all day. He worked at the same job for thirty years. There was usually a garden to provide vegetables. The mom stayed at home with the kids. She made the ship run and tried to make sure dinner was on the table when the dad came home.

Our family was no different. It's just that my dad was a pastor. We did our best to make ends meet. Life was hard, but it was good. Kids usually pursued the same occupations as their parents—even if it meant working in the local factory. With my dad as a pastor, all five of my siblings entered the ministry in some shape or form.

When we were growing up, the entire family worked together. The family garden was a group project. Preserving and canning the vegetables meant that we'd have food in the winter. We'd go pick cotton together and pool our money to buy something we needed for the house. We all got jobs as soon as we could and started paying our own way to take pressure off the family finances. Even when I started working in high school, I was contributing part of my income to the household.

We played together. We prayed together. Church was Sunday morning, Sunday evening, and Wednesday evening.

When Barbara and I got married, we skimped and saved to buy our first house. We tithed off our $60 paycheck, and slowly but surely, with every promotion, we made advances as a family. By 1970, we started our own business in our garage—even that was a family affair. We made picture frames. Mart and Steve glued frames together, and we paid them seven cents for each frame. Barbara was the shipping department and shipped them to our customers. When we opened our first store in 1972, Barbara was the one to run it. When we opened our second store, I quit my job at TG&Y, cut my salary in half, and went to work full-time in the business. Even with all this start-up effort, my goal was to be home every night for dinner.

Why do I spend so much time with this history? This is not just a trip down memory lane. And it's not to say that the era I grew up in was better. Instead, that season of time reflected a certain worldview of the family.

Family was at the center of everything. We worked as a team. We needed to—we depended on every member to play a vital role in the life of the family. Dad was the worker; my mom was right alongside him in ministry and in taking care of the house. As kids, we were contributing members as well. It wasn't a question of whether we wanted to help. We had to help. If everyone didn't contribute, we wouldn't make it. We were interdependent. We all had to sacrifice our own individual needs and desires. Individual sports and hobbies weren't an option.

At the core of our family was a deep faith too. That faith kept us focused. As a family, we had a greater calling. We weren't just in it for ourselves. On the wall of our home was a simple cross-stitched portion of a poem by C. T. Studd:

> Only one life, 'twill soon be past,
> Only what's done for Christ will last.

Looking back, I realize that was our family motto. Our family was focused on eternity. We learned that family was more important than any one individual.

Now trust me, I'm not trying to say our family was perfect. We weren't. As you look at my own experience, I think it's important to take a step back and look at the larger picture of family in our country.

A Brief History of Family

A Cultural View of Family History

The history of family in our country tells us a lot about where we stand with our family worldview. Dennis Jaffe in *Borrowed from Your Grandchildren: The Evolution of 100-Year Family Enterprises* provides a quick synopsis of the history of family:[1]

1. In the beginning, the family was the only unit in society. Family served as the school, the economy, the values teacher, and the church all rolled into one.
2. Every family was effectively a business. They had to be.

3. With the rise of agriculture and farming, families settled together and formed roots in communities.
4. Families formed clans, then tribes, then alliances, which turned into villages and cities. These family units were highly interdependent and multigenerational.
5. "While each family's business was important, *the core was the family*—its values and resources as well as the people who emerged in each generation to move it forward."
6. An essential element of family thriving was the investment in children and their futures. Family success was viewed as a multigenerational project.

A Biblical View of Family History

The history Jaffe outlines is consistent with the biblical narrative. In Genesis, the family is the first institution that God establishes by way of Adam and Eve. Their mission was to "be fruitful and increase in number; fill the earth and subdue it"—to make the world more beautiful and creative (1:26–28).

After the fall, the biblical record shows that Adam and the succeeding generations lived long lives. That longevity means that Adam was alive to see at least the seventh generation of his family.[2] It is not inconceivable (in fact, it is likely) that Adam was having conversations with his great-great-great-great-great-grandchildren about the blessing of life in the garden—a life at peace with God the Father.[3] You can almost imagine Adam telling his generations of descendants, "We must get back to Eden."

By Genesis 12, God has moved His focus to one family, Abraham and Sarah, where He promises to give them a land, make them a great nation, and make them a blessing to the world. Once again, Abraham and Sarah are back at the stage where they are highly interdependent on each other and wholly dependent on the Lord—the place He wants us to be.

The Industrial Age and the Impact on the Family

This highly interdependent state of the family declines as the family moves away from the farm. Industrialization leads to significant changes for the family. Krishan Kumar, in his article "Work and the Family," provides an excellent summary of these effects:

1. Families become smaller; children are no longer needed for labor.
2. The family moves away from functioning as an independent community, where the family is at the center of religious, educational, social, and economic life.
3. Instead, the family's primary role becomes child-raising, but even that role fades to the background, giving way to external organized structures (school, friends, youth group, day care, etc.) and social media.
4. As a result, the values of children are shaped more by outside influences than the home.
5. The ultimate aim becomes finding identity in work and career and spending your earnings on your own pleasures versus the good of the family.

6. Kumar writes, "Modernization involves a process of secularization; that is, it systematically challenges religious institutions, beliefs, and practices, substituting for them those of reason and science."[4]

Do you follow the track? With the rise of industrialization, the family takes a back seat to business. Kumar summarizes his article by saying, "The decline of religion and community removes the traditional restraints on appetite, allowing it to grow morbidly and without limit. At the same time the competitive modern order that stimulates these unreal expectations provides insufficient and unequal means for their realization. The result is an increase in suicide, crime and mental disorders."[5] Put differently, we are focused on ourselves and what gain we may have as individuals rather than the larger good of the community.

It is not enough to read this history of the family and accept it for what it is. Instead, we need to diagnose this history and ask ourselves: What happened?

What Went Wrong?

As you read this simplified history of family, some obvious factors stand out. We started out with family in the center of our world. Family was literally everything. The school, the church, the business, the primary emphasis of socialization. We worked together for the good of the family. We needed each other. We found our identity in the life of family.

But over time, as we moved away from the farm and into a modern industrialized society, our families got smaller. The family moved out of the center, and instead our work life became our identity. Family became the place where we raised our kids but not much else. And some of those family duties became delegated to the school, to the church, to the Little League, to the babysitter, or to the day care. Family was in competition with these other spheres of influence. It certainly was no longer the central influence.

> We allowed culture to define the family instead of the Bible.

As the family moved out of the center stage, the emphasis became on the wants and needs of the individual. The focus became on upward mobility—what kind of lifestyle I can live, what I can buy, what I can own. "Enjoy this short life while you can" became an underlying philosophy. No longer was family and community the first driver.

As you read this short summary of the family's decline, please don't miss the message. The rise and fall of the family might be stated simply:

We allowed culture to define the family instead of the Bible.

As we fed our families through the gristmill of cultural forces, what emerged was something vastly different from God's design. God intended for the family to be the center of influence, the values teacher, and the place of safety—where the family advanced as a team to accomplish God's plan for them in the world. God's design was not for all the functions of family to be delegated to outside agencies.

If there's any doubt about this gradual descent over time, just consider how family has been portrayed on television over the decades. Take a look:

1954: *Father Knows Best*—A wise father and sensible mother guide their three children in navigating life.[6]

1957: *Leave It to Beaver*—A young boy grows up in his nuclear family, guided by both parents as he navigates life.[7]

1960: *My Three Sons*—A widower raises three sons with the help of his father-in-law and great-uncle.[8]

1972: *The Waltons*—A married couple with seven children and their grandparents live in a small mountain town.[9]

Each of these shows generally had a strong father figure, a mother, and children living in unity as a family. But then by the 1990s and 2000s,[10] we had television shows like:

1987: *Married . . . with Children*—This family was dysfunctional at every level and centered on a bumbling, ineffective dad.

1989: *Seinfeld*—A show self-described to be literally about nothing, with single adults disconnected from their own family units.

1994: *Friends*—Twenty- and thirtysomething friends alienated from their own families form their own community.

2009: *Modern Family*—Three family types (nuclear, blended, and adoptive/gay) live out family life.

Up to this point, I've not touched upon the faith of families. It should not surprise us that as the family has declined, so has faith. The Pew Research Center has studied the ongoing decline in religious life in America. Their findings include the following:

- 80 percent of Americans say that the influence of faith is shrinking.[11]
- Although 65 percent of Americans describe themselves as Christians, that number shows a 12 percent decline in a decade.[12]
- Meanwhile, the rise of the nones—the religiously unaffiliated—is up to 26 percent.[13]

Mary Eberstadt says it this way in *How the West Really Lost God: A New Theory of Secularization*:

> Like the waning of Christianity, the waning of the traditional family means that all of us in the modern West lead lives our ancestors could not have imagined. We are less fettered than they in innumerable ways; we are perhaps the freest people in the history of the world. At the same time, we are also more deprived of the consolations of the tight bonds of family and faith known to most of the men and women coming before us.[14]

Quite simply, as the family goes, so goes faith. As the family declines, so does faith. With this history and background, we can better state where we stand with our family worldview—call it our family theology—in today's world. Many of these concepts are tackled in Jeremy Pryor's book *Family Revision: How Ancient Wisdom Can Heal the Modern Family* and provide a good framework for the discussion.

There, the author compares the Western family with what he calls the classical family.[15]

Family Worldview Today

So where do we stand today with family? Our Western culture's view of family, children, and parenting has drifted from a biblical view to an individualistic view.

Today, most families would see themselves as a nest. As long as our children are in the nest, we'll feed them, protect them, and try to do the right things for them. We'll do all that we can to make sure they get the best food, the best clothes, the best education. We'll go the extra mile for them to make sure they get the best experiences—sports teams, music lessons, vacations, academic tutoring, and so on. We'll wait anxiously to see if they made the top teams. And we'll pile on experience after experience, trying to make sure they don't miss out. With all this focus on children, it can seem we are family focused. But we're not. Kids are at the center of the world—not the family.

This child-centered parenting has the impact of teaching kids that the world is about them. The accomplishments of the individual are more important than the accomplishments of the family, the community, and the church.

Because of this attention on the individual, our perspective of kids is that they are expensive. If we are going to fund all their needs, including college, then those bills will add up. As a result, we shouldn't have too many. In this environment, siblings are often competing for resources—the attention of parents, the allocation of resources to "their" activities.

And marriage? In Western culture, the wife usually leads the family, and the husband focuses on his career. He is involved in the family but draws his main identity from work. Pryor writes, "Today a man could have an amazing career, leave his family in ruins and still be considered a truly great man."[16] He works hard in business and then is expected to love his family as an afterthought to building a great career.

And as we saw in the television shows listed earlier, often the media depicts fathers as emotionally unaware or awkward. The mom takes the helm in guiding the family, and the father focuses on leading in his career.

But in the biblical model, the wife leads in partnership with her husband. And the father is the one burdened with the primary responsibility: "Fathers, do not exasperate your children; instead, bring them up in the training and instruction of the Lord" (Eph. 6:4). In the biblical model, before life became so separated, kids worked alongside parents as a team, and spouses worked together as a team, with the primary responsibility of raising children falling on the husband.

How do we measure success in the nest model? It's the success of the individual. The honor society. State championships. Music awards. Good grades. Scholarships. Finances. Pause for a moment and think about kingdom success. My mom and dad would not have been considered a worldly success. But they advanced the gospel with their lives and the lives of their family.

What's the goal of this nest for family? It's an empty nest. We'll do all we can to prepare our children for life outside the nest. In fact, many jest today that they've "got the kids off the payroll." Now, don't misunderstand, I'm not suggesting that our adult children are still supposed to be living in our basements. That's a failure to launch. What I am saying is there was a time when our families lived under a mission and mandate together—to make the world a more beautiful and creative place in the character and image of God.

For parents, when we get to the empty-nest stage of life, we can pursue our own goals. For moms, it may be that they go back to work, go back to school, or pursue that long-awaited hobby. For dads, it may mean retirement, travel, more golf—or pickleball! These other pursuits by nature mean that the parents become unavailable except for occasional grandparenting duty.

The problem with this empty-nest worldview is that it promotes and encourages a hyper-individualistic culture at every level. For the kids. For the parents. For the grandparents. We don't stand for anything as a family other than our own individual interests. We break into a thousand little pieces.

Here's a quick summary of the differences I see between a cultural worldview and a biblical worldview:

Issue	Cultural Worldview	Biblical Worldview
Family unit	Family as a nest	Family as a team
Goal for children	Independence	Interdependence
Goal for parents	Empty nest	Ongoing engagement with children and grandchildren
Goal of father	Find identity at work	Find identity in success of family first
Goal of mother	Do it all! Lead in child-raising	Lead in partnership with the husband
Family business	Exit or sell	Steward and sustain

Where Do We Go from Here?

As a culture, our families are neck-deep in hyper-individualism. But what would culture look like if family and community came first? What if "we" came before "me"?

We would choose to stay interdependent by necessity.

This is why Barbara and I haven't sold Hobby Lobby and retired in Florida. We could have gone that route. But we believe we are still on a mission as a family. Years ago, I realized that the business belongs to God. It serves a far greater purpose than just making money. It exists to win souls.

Do you see the difference? When we choose to stay interdependent, even after prosperity, we recognize that other people need us and that we need them. This is God's plan.

On a spiritual level, we need each other. Paul writes in Ephesians, "From [Jesus] the whole body, joined and held together by every supporting ligament, grows and builds itself up in love, as each part does its work" (4:16). We grow and build each other up. Each part plays a role.

Don't dismiss this if you live alone or don't have children. You are likely still a brother or sister, a daughter or son, an uncle or aunt. And you are always a member of the family of God. You fill a greater role beyond looking out for yourself. You belong to a team—a team that needs you. Pryor says it like this: "Each family member is seen as part of a cohesive team."[17]

In his book *How to Tell the Truth*, author and evangelist Preston Perry shares his story of coming to Christ.[18] He grew up in South Chicago, and his grandma showed him a love for God. His neighbor led a house church in a nearby apartment. Preston received enough exposure to church to know that he didn't know God. He lived a life of crime until he saw one of his friends get shot and pass away in his arms. After that moment, Preston knew he had to leave his life of crime, but all of his friends lived that way, so he went to live with his aunt. She prayed for him every day and introduced him to a college student and former gang member from another neighborhood in Chicago, who showed Preston what it meant to know God. Preston realized God was chasing him down. He gave his heart to Christ.

Think of all the people involved in his journey—the grandma. The neighbor. The aunt. The college student. Each played a role. Each sacrificed their "me" for Preston and those like him.

Are you on the team?

Or are you caught up in trying to build a life you love? Jesus warns us, "Unless a kernel of wheat falls to the ground and dies, it remains only a single seed. But if it dies, it produces many seeds" (John 12:24).

The beauty of an individual seed that dies to itself is that it bears much fruit. What do you want to be? Let's take the next step and talk about the practices that will help you be the seed that dies and lives the Legacy Life.

PART 2
LEGACY PRACTICES

5

SETTING YOUR COURSE

Suppose one of you wants to build a tower. Won't you first sit down and estimate the cost to see if you have enough money to complete it?

Luke 14:28

What does it take to live the Legacy Life? What does it take for your life and your family to thrive for generations to come?

By part 2 of this book, you should have down the concept that legacy is what you set in motion. But we think too shortterm. No, indeed, for our lives and our family, we should be thinking in terms of generations of impact and influence. However, we must not let the world's culture define our lives and our families. We must recognize that God's design for our lives is truly generational in nature.

Here, in part 2, we'll turn practical. How do you live the Legacy Life? What are the practical steps we must take to live out that kind of life? Before we go there, some of you might be asking, "Now wait a minute, does this really work?"

Is Generational Success Possible—*Really*?

I'd like to layer on some academic study of the issue. In the last chapter, I mentioned Dennis Jaffe and the work that he's done studying what he calls the one-hundred-year family. Over time, Jaffe has gone back and studied those families who have had generational success. He interviewed them and culled their best practices.

His work parallels the work of James Hughes, who wrote the foundational book *Family Wealth—Keeping It in the Family*.[1] Hughes is one of the well-recognized leaders in working with multigenerational families. By the way, when you hear the term *wealth*, be careful to recognize that Hughes and others in this generational success area rightly define *wealth* more broadly than money and finance. While Hughes defines *wealth* as human, intellectual, and financial capital, I define it similarly but differently.[2] From my point of view, wealth is intellectual, social, emotional, financial, and *spiritual*.

But the central theme of Jaffe's and Hughes' studies is whether a family can preserve its wealth (defined broadly) for four generations or more.[3] The short answer from both is a simple yes.

Let me offer a brief caveat. The Jaffe and Hughes studies arise out of those families who have a business or a family office. Once again, don't misunderstand: This is not a book about business. This is a book about generational success. Jaffe and Hughes both underscore that to achieve generational success, *the family* must first be healthy and thriving. The main point is that a family must have a reason to be—a reason that they exist. The reason to exist must inherently be a values-driven discussion. Families who follow Christ should have the greatest reason to work toward generational success.

So, what are some of those practices for generational success?

Practices for Generational Success

The research and work from Jaffe and Hughes land largely at the same place for generational success. I share their research here because their mindset of investing in family with an outlook of four generations or more is so rare. However, these truths apply to more than just families. Wherever you are, whatever stage of life you are in, the key is to be intentional about how you live your life.

Jaffe points out that great families develop a family vision, a great culture, and family values.[4] More precisely, "Each family enterprise must define its purpose and practices, its mission, values, and governance."[5] Each successive generation must affirm and reaffirm these purposes and practices.[6]

> **Great families develop a family vision, a great culture, and family values.**

Hughes says it slightly differently: "A family must form a social compact among its members reflecting its shared values, and each successive generation must reaffirm and readopt that social compact."[7] He also emphasizes the need for families to recognize that they must continue to be creators of wealth in all forms. And it is really hard work. You must be intentional and have a long-term mindset.[8]

In context, Jaffe and Hughes reflect the same ideas we discussed in chapter 3 related to God's generational design. These principles can be summed up with Psalm 145:4: "One generation shall commend your works to another, and shall declare your mighty acts" (ESV).

While the Jaffe and Hughes books weren't around when we got married, from the earliest days of our relationship, Barbara and I always wanted to make sure that we'd have a great marriage and a great family. As I look back now with hindsight, I see a few keys for us. Once again, let me pause here and issue my disclaimer: We are not a perfect family, and we always have things to get better at! We are working toward that goal of 150 years or more.

First, we operated with a stewardship mindset. Coming from the poor background that I did, I always felt so blessed by all God had put in my hands—my wife, my children, the ministry of my work and all the relationships that came with that. That stewardship mindset extended to our company. We always taught our children that God is the owner of the business—not us. We never took profit out of the company to spend on ourselves. We believed that we should continue to invest in growth so that we could best invest in God's kingdom.

Interestingly, both Jaffe and Hughes speak with a similar mindset, although they say it in different ways. Jaffe speaks of the idea that we don't own companies (or anything that we have, for that matter). Instead, we borrow it from our grandchildren. Hughes gets at the same idea by saying that every generation must see itself as the first generation. The idea is that we are always working to hand it off to future generations and not just spend it on ourselves.

Second, consistent with that stewardship mindset, we always practiced giving as a family. Not only did we see this practice in our parents, but we taught our children to be givers as well. By teaching giving, we teach our children and grandchildren that life is not about us. We could spend more on ourselves, but why? There's a world out there that still doesn't know Jesus. That generous lifestyle cuts against the selfish, individualistic world we live in. And notably, it's important that you include your children in the discussion and the activity. Too many families have not included their children in the giving discussion.

A third key practice is the concept of a family giving meeting. Twenty-five years ago, we began meeting monthly as a family (my wife Barbara, our children and their spouses, and our nephew Randy) to talk about our giving. Our grandchildren join us in those meetings even though they don't yet have a vote. This allows them to observe the process because one day they may have an opportunity to sit in our seats. We begin our meetings with Scripture and prayer. We review requests, discuss them, and vote on how much to give. We always end our meetings with the "story of one"—a story about how our giving has impacted the life of an individual. And we close with a celebration song. It is a fun and neat way for us to live out our family values monthly.

A fourth key practice was that we clearly defined our family vision, mission, and values. While I often joke about Bill, my coauthor, I tell people that his parents were so wise that they knew he was going to be an attorney someday because they gave him the perfect lawyer name: Bill High. If you have ever worked with attorneys, then you know what I mean. I fear that one day Bill will open a law firm and call it "Biller High!" Alas, I digress again.

Anyhow, Bill's work and ministry is to help families work toward generational success. While we already had a clear sense of who we were as a family, Bill corralled our family and worked with us over a period of months to write down on paper our 150-year vision statement, our mission statement, and our family values.

> Our vision: To go on the adventure of impacting our world for Christ.
> Our mission: To love God intimately. To live extravagant generosity.
> Our values: God, family, others.

That work of defining family vision, mission, and values led to one of our other key practices: family celebration. On a smaller scale, we try to gather as many of our forty-plus family members as possible on a quarterly basis to celebrate birthdays. During that time, we want to offer words of affirmation for those who have had birthdays during that quarter.

However, on an annual basis, we also have a family celebration. During that celebration, we want to renew our commitment to our vision, mission, and values as a family. In the past, the celebrations have been led by our children, and now each of the grandchildren have led these celebrations. This allows each family unit to uniquely express those values.

As part of that celebration, we've also printed a one-of-a-kind family Bible that members receive when they come of age (at sixteen) to join the celebration. We are not far from having our first fourth-generation family member join!

Whether you live with family members or live on your own, the key here is to be intentional. Set aside regular times to review your vision, mission, and values and to remember what God has done.

Why Family Vision, Mission, and Values?

I've always said that it is far easier to run a business than it is to run a family. Even in our personal lives, whether or not we have families of our own, often our best intentions go toward building our careers instead of planning for long-term impact. We'll spend thousands of dollars hiring consultants to help our companies, churches, and nonprofits develop vision, mission, and values statements. Yet we won't undergo the same time commitment for our families and personal lives. But let me share one quick story illustrating why this is so important.

On July 4, 1952, Florence Chadwick plunged into the ice-cold Pacific Ocean and began to swim.[9] She was the first woman who tried to swim the twenty-one miles between Catalina Island and the coast of California. For hours, she fought through the chilly, choppy waters of the Pacific. Her boat crew spotted sharks circling nearby and occasionally fired shots into the ocean to scare them away. Florence kept swimming. Her mother rode in one of the boats, shouting words of encouragement. Fifteen hours in, the fog hung so dense Florence could hardly see the boat just behind her.

Florence persevered another hour, then called for the boat. She quit. After climbing in, she discovered that she was less than a mile from reaching the shore.

Florence later told a reporter, "I think if I could have seen the shore, I would have made it."

> "If I could have seen the shore, I would have made it."
> —Florence Chadwick

So many of us start off in our youth full of confidence and vigor. We endeavor to pilot our ship to a place of warmth, comfort, and greatness.

But, somewhere along the way, reality enters. The destination seems less clear. The fog rolls in, and we can't see the shoreline that once seemed so clear. Here's the stark truth:

If we don't have a picture of the shoreline, we will likely quit.

Vision pulls us onward. Vision whispers we can keep going, no matter the challenges we face or the difficulty of the course. If we don't have vision, we will quit.

Developing Your Vision, Mission, and Values

My hope is that as you read these words, you'll not just be inspired, but you'll take the next step and develop your own vision, mission, and values statement for your life and your family. As Jonathan Swift is attributed as saying, "Vision is the art of seeing what is invisible to others." Do you have a clear picture of the shoreline? If you don't know where you are headed, you will never arrive. Sure, you will arrive somewhere, but it won't be the place you wanted to go. Proverbs

4:26 encourages us, "Give careful thought to the paths for your feet and be steadfast in all your ways."

Here's the instruction Bill gives to those who participate in his workshops: Develop your vision statement by writing down a short, concise statement—five to seven words. If you can't remember it, then you won't use it. But the statement has got to be big and exciting and use big words like *generations, every, everywhere, thousands,* and so on. Some of the vision statements come straight out of the Bible:

Taking the gospel to every nation.

Disciples everywhere for generations.

Every generation serving Christ.

If you need some help, visit Bill's website at Legacy Stone (LegacyStone.com) for samples that you are free to borrow as your own.

Not only do individuals and families need a big picture of the future—the vision statement—but they also need a mission statement. A mission statement is a practical statement of action. This action helps accomplish the vision.

The mission isn't exciting or glamorous. It's just practical instruction. Having a short statement allows for daily repetition. It's in the memorization—in the rinse and repeat—that the power lies. Once again, many of these can be taken straight out of the Bible:

Seek first His kingdom daily.

Love God. Love people. Serve the world.

Trust in the Lord with all your heart.
Read the Word. Obey God's Word.

You get the idea. The practical instruction of a mission statement can sit and dwell not only in our own hearts but in the lives of our children. These simple mantras become like the melody of a good song you can't get out of your head.

The final step in setting your course toward the Legacy Life is a clear set of personal and family values.

Values are personal principles of behavior. They are the guardrails to life. They help keep us in our lanes, and they tell us when we are going out of bounds. They are the compass settings that keep the ship on track. They are the glue that keeps a family together. In the appendix to this book (found on page 195), we'll include examples of values. But generally, identify three to five values that you'd like to live out and teach to your family on an ongoing basis. These values might look something like this:

Faith
Family
Integrity
Gratitude
Generosity

The power of values is that they are both protective and attractive for the generations. They teach us our identity—who we are not and who we are. Will you take the time to write down your vision, mission, and values statement for you and your family?

Putting It into Practice

There's a popular adage that values are caught, not taught. The idea is that if you don't model your values, then they will never be reflected in your children. While it's true that values must be modeled, it is also true that if they are never clearly articulated, then they will not be captured and lived out by your children.

Deuteronomy 6:6–9 says, "These commandments that I give you today are to be on your hearts. Impress them on your children. Talk about them when you sit at home and when you walk along the road, when you lie down and when you get up. Tie them as symbols on your hands and bind them on your foreheads. Write them on the doorframes of your houses and on your gates."

Does it sound like the commandments are caught or taught? Impress them. Talk about them. Tie them. Bind them. Write them. To me, those phrases sure sound like teaching—constantly. Barbara and I lived out our values by example, but we also talked about them. We told our children why prayer is so important, why God wants full obedience, and why we can lean on His Word daily. We modeled values and we taught them too.

Does this work? Let me give you a few examples of people living this out now.

One family, Micah and Audrey McElveen, who we met through our events at Hobby Lobby and who also attended one of Bill's workshops, came back to us with these stories. During the workshop, they prayed over and crafted their own vision, mission, and values statements. They run a ministry called Vapor Ministries, and they knew that their vision, mission, and values would relate to reaching souls. Here are their statements:

> Vision: Touch millions together. Raise Jesus forever.
> Mission: Serve souls. Praise God.
> Values: Chase God. Stand strong. Love our crew. Embrace others.

They went home and asked their kids to sign the statements. They printed the statements on a canvas and hung it in their living room. They painted symbols representing their mission around their house. They stuck a copy of their statements on their fridge. They even made pillowcases with Bible verses reflecting the values. Every night at bedtime, they choose a value and talk about how they saw family members living it out that day.

Their children were four and two years old when they created the statements. But Micah and Audrey soon realized that when the kids went to school, much of their time would be spent outside the home. Micah and Audrey wanted their children to remember their identity all day at school. So, they turned the vision and values into a rallying chant they say together every morning before school. And now Micah and Audrey come back to us with stories of their children living it out.

But what if you don't have kids? One young couple, Luis and Kaytlynn Magaña, attended a workshop Bill had led on family legacy while they were engaged. They created their vision statement: "Magnifying Christ and enjoying one another forever." They wrote out their mission: "Pursue kindness, love joyfully, and walk humbly with the Lord." They started dreaming of creating their own 150-year family legacy through their family. Then they got married, and soon infertility issues forced them to consider the prospect that they might never be able to have children. They had dreamed of being able to shape a legacy. But what would legacy look like without kids? They realized their family legacy might look like adoption or fostering. Even if they only fostered a child for a short time, their impact could still carry on through that child for generations to come.

Ken Polk received a similar challenge early in his career. He had devoted much time to launching his own business, maintaining clients, and building out their portfolios. Then one day, a question in a book stopped him short. He read, "Are you saving your best thinking for your business or your family?"

Ken realized he was spending long days taking care of his clients but not investing the same mental energy in his family. He and his wife Ashley started creating systems for their family to thrive, just as Ken had for his business. They created a family vision: "God first, family next." From there, they wrote out their values: "Be honest, be excellent, be disciplined." They carried out regular family meetings with their four children, and as the children grew, they internalized the values and began challenging their parents in return.

Over the years, they've had many opportunities to practice this, which has led to humorous stories as a family. Ken gets to utilize these same practices now with his clients at Arlington Family Offices.[10]

Bill's friends Dustin and Noelle Doll are on a similar journey. With three kids, they work out their family vision, mission, and values through regular family meetings. They take time to discuss issues, and they ask their kids to bring up any concerns. And the kids do bring up concerns. One time they told Dustin he was spending too much time on his phone. They came up with a family plan that involved Dustin putting his phone in a locked cookie jar for a certain amount of time each day after work. The vision and mission gave his family a goal to work toward, and the family meetings provided the structure to see the vision come to life.

Whatever your life situation, if you want to set a great legacy in motion, your practices will determine your success. In the next chapter, we'll tackle the concept of a code of conduct.

6

LIVING *by a* CODE *of* CONDUCT

Well, if no one among us is capable of governing himself, then who among us has the capacity to govern someone else?

Ronald Reagan

The Legacy Life happens only with intentionality. Some might call it the championship kind of life.

What does it take to live a championship kind of life? John Wooden knew; he was a champion at every level of his life.

John played basketball for Purdue University, where he was an All-American for three seasons.[1] He coached high school basketball before serving in the Navy during World War II. Afterward, he coached basketball at Indiana State before moving to UCLA. There, he made his mark: He won an unprecedented ten national championships. During forty years of coaching, he won 885 games, with a career winning percentage of 81. He's the only person to be inducted into the players' and coaches' Hall of Fame.[2]

What was the key to Wooden's success?

When John graduated from elementary school, his father gave him an index card with an inspirational saying written on the front and a code of conduct on the back. John kept this card folded in his wallet throughout his life, and it became his "Seven-Point Creed." The back of the card showed the following code:

Seven Things to Do
1. Be true to yourself.
2. Help others.
3. Make each day your masterpiece.
4. Drink deeply from good books, especially the Bible.
5. Make friendship a fine art.
6. Build a shelter against a rainy day.
7. Pray for guidance and count and give thanks for your blessings every day.[3]

John kept this constantly by his side and aimed to live it out. As we look at his life, we can see that he did.

John Wooden lived intentionally. He learned to govern himself.

Like John Wooden, you can move toward living a meaningful life by determining the rules by which you'll live—some call it a code of conduct. A code of conduct guides our actions. Every day we make hundreds of choices, and we can easily forget our lofty ideals in life's mundanity. A code takes those ideals, or values, that can seem high-level and turns them into daily guidance.

The Concept of a Code of Conduct

The idea of a code of conduct is not new. If you take a quick scan, you'll find that virtually every profession has a code: medicine, law, engineering, accounting, military, banking, and so on. Even cowboys had a code. Some call it the code of the West.[4] I'll articulate my summary of it.

- Be tough but fair.
- Do your job. Do it right.
- Defend the weak.
- Finish what you start.
- Live with courage.
- Do what you say.

The code of the West guided the cowboy. Cowboys had a code to live by that made them different from others. They stood out. In medieval times, the knights had their own code, and in modern times, the Navy SEALs have a strict code of conduct as well.

In the business world, we see the same idea. The Kikkoman soy sauce family is in their twentieth generation. They've been living by some basic rules for a hundred years. Some of their code includes the following:

- Strive for harmony in your family.
- Avoid luxury: A simple life is a virtuous life.

- Do the job you were born to do, and only that job.
- Eat the same food as your servants.
- Keep your personal expenses low.[5]

Or consider the Kongō Gumi family. They operated one of the oldest family-owned businesses in the world. They had a similar code, which they called their creed. Here's part of it:

- Give each task your full attention.
- Don't diversify. Concentrate on your core business.
- Be well-mannered and humble and respect status.
- Respect others and listen to what they say, but don't be overly influenced by their words.
- Always use common sense.[6]

The Power and Purpose of the Code of Conduct

What's the purpose of a code of conduct?

A code provides a definition, a guideline for how people should act in their profession or company. You may choose to call it your rule of life or rules to live by, but these rules are particularly powerful when implemented in your individual life and in the life of your family.

Jonathan Edwards and Max Jukes provide a sharp contrast of two men of the same era with vastly different results.

Jonathan Edwards was a well-known Puritan preacher during the 1700s who later became president of Princeton University. He and his wife Sarah had eleven children. An American educator named A. E. Winship decided to trace Edwards's lineage 150 years after his death. He found that the Edwards's family tree included one hundred pastors, one hundred lawyers, sixty doctors, sixty-five professors, thirteen mayors, seventy-five military officers, one US vice president, three US senators, and three governors.[7]

In contrast, in 1877, Richard Dugdale, a sociologist, studied the family trees of forty-two men in the New York prison system. These men were traced back to Max Jukes. His descendants included "7 murderers, 60 thieves, 190 prostitutes, 150 other convicts, 310 paupers, and 440" alcoholics.[8]

What contributed to the difference in the legacy of these two men?

When Edwards was still a teenager, he developed a series of resolutions—a code—to live by. He went over these resolutions on a weekly basis. His code included resolutions like these:

- I will do whatever I think will be most to God's glory.
- Never lose one moment of time; but seize the time to use it in the most profitable way I possibly can.
- To live with all my might . . . while I do live.
- Never to do anything which I would be afraid to do if it were the last hour of my life.
- To think much, on all occasions, about my own dying, and of the common things which are involved with and surround death.
- To maintain the wisest and healthiest practices in my eating and drinking.[9]

Edwards reviewed these resolutions on a weekly, monthly, and yearly basis.[10] Also, as part of his daily practice, he would talk for an hour with his children and wife and pray a blessing over each of his children.[11]

The practice of your own code, resolutions, or rules to live by becomes a powerful tool not only for yourself but for your family as well. The code provides accountability for how we live and act in relationship with one another.

My Personal Code

Unlike Jonathan Edwards, I did not develop my code when I was in my teens, although I wish I'd had the foresight to have done so. My code developed over time. The start of that code comes out of my own weakness. There was a time in business when I ruled with authority. Because I was the CEO, I could use my position to get what I wanted. I'm not proud of it, but there was a time when we were looking for a particular store location. Things didn't seem to be happening fast enough, or maybe we weren't doing enough to acquire it. As a result, I remember demanding of my real estate manager that "he better do all that he could to get the deal done." The implicit threat of "or else" hung in the air.

It was during this season that God gave me my first rule in my code of conduct. I was trying too hard to make things happen, and it seemed that I was pushing everything uphill and testing my own values. While I was away on a business trip, I remember feeling down and low—disappointed with myself. God brought Psalm 24:3–4 to mind: "Who may ascend the mountain of the LORD? Who may stand in his holy place? The one who has clean hands and a pure heart."

I realized then and there that I was called to a higher standard in every aspect of my life—a life of integrity, to honor

God in all that I do. Since that time, that rule—clean hands and a pure heart—is my number one rule. My next three, all coming straight from Scripture, reflect the way that I want to live my daily life:

1. *Jesus is always with me. He will never leave me or forsake me.* This comes straight from Deuteronomy 31:8: "The LORD himself goes before you and will be with you; he will never leave you nor forsake you." This verse reminds me that Jesus is right beside me, so I can walk and talk with Him daily, which leads to my next rule.
2. *Pray without ceasing.* This rule is based upon 1 Thessalonians 5:17. If Jesus is always with me, then I can constantly pray and ask Him for help in everything going on in my day. I believe that when we reach a point in our lives where we think we don't need God's help on a moment-by-moment basis, then we are at risk of running our own lives. But let me also say that I *try* to pray without ceasing. It's something I'll be working at the rest of my life.
3. *Ask and you'll receive. You have not because you ask not.* This rule is based upon Matthew 7:7 and James 4:3–4. I'll note that James reminds us to ask with the right motives. If my prayer is to make Hobby Lobby more profitable just so I can buy a boat, well, that's not a right motive. But if my prayer is for wisdom so that more people can hear the gospel, then I'm heading in the right direction.

Call it what you'd like—code of conduct or rules to live by. But I know that when you have a set of principles like this and you remind yourself of those principles—like John Wooden did—you stand a greater chance of living a Legacy Life. And you'll be less likely to be so hard on those in your care.

What Should Be in Your Code?

Those who live the Legacy Life are those who live by a clear code. Are you ready to write yours?

Okay, let me take the pressure off. You don't need to write the US Constitution. And you don't have to write your own set of laws. But you can take the patterns of what God has given us in the Scriptures as a guide to writing your own code.

As Bill and I have worked with leaders, we have found that although the Bible gives many guiding principles, it is helpful for them to write out their own version of a code of conduct. Here are some basic elements of your code:

1. How will you live toward God?
2. How will you live toward your family?
3. How will you live toward others?

Remember that your code will fit in with your vision, mission, and values statements.

Vision paints the picture of your life and your family for the next 150 years. It contains big, bold dreams—an adventurous kind of statement. Take the land. Claim a nation. Rebuild the walls. Release the captives.

The mission is the high-level statement of what you will do to accomplish the vision. Ask, seek, pray. Trust in the Lord. It encompasses the repetitive action of the faithful.

Values answer *why* you want these things. They are the single words that represent what your heart longs for and clings to—for example, faith, grit, hope, sacrifice.

And the code of conduct is the specific statements that describe your behaviors (e.g., "We live in faith by seeking God daily in His Word and praying"). They provide practical guidance and structures for growth. They become the trellis that can guide future generations long after you are gone.

As Bill leads workshops, he has seen families changed by creating a code of conduct. Don and Carla Wenner created what they call their family compass, combining each of their values with a statement for how to live it out daily. First, they wrote out their vision: "Every generation making a 100x impact." Then they created their mission: "Lead with love and intentional action to light up the world." Afterward, they wrote out their values and code of conduct together as an acronym to "Be a light." Here's an abbreviated version of their values and code:

Be Present. Enjoy the moment with an attitude of gratitude.

Authentic. Maintain and display humble confidence.

Live Fully. Maximize each day and the blessings the Lord has provided.

Impact. Give time, talent, and treasures generously.

Grit and Growth. Persevere toward long-term goals with curiosity and a desire to grow.

Honor God. Through servant leadership to the Lord, to family, and at work.

Tribe. Build thriving relationships through our relationship with the Lord.

They have hung their compass in every bedroom, in the kitchen, and in the living room. They teach the principles to their children regularly.

To share their value of "grit and growth," they talked with their sons about persevering through setbacks and always seeing challenges as opportunities to grow and overcome obstacles. As their boys have grown, Don has started hearing comments reflecting this value in daily life. On the basketball court, if his son misses a play, he'll say, "I'm not worried about it. I have grit." Or while studying Spanish: "I'm not good at Spanish now, but I have no doubt I can get really good." Talking regularly about a code of conduct translates into daily life. The values represent the ideal, and the code shows how to live them out.

As we mentioned earlier, Luis and Kaytlynn Magaña attended a workshop while newly engaged, and they created a code of conduct together before getting married. The code has guided them through the common conflicts of any new marriage, and they return to their code almost daily. It includes phrases like "We forgive early" and "We are on the same team." When struggles arise, the code of conduct reorients them quickly and keeps them united. It brings their ideals into daily life.

A People Set Apart

There's one more big idea about the code of conduct. Bill tells me the story of one time when he was riding in an Uber where the driver had a handcrafted leatherbound Bible on his dashboard. Bill asked, "Do you read it?" The driver was cautious, and said, "Yes, every single day." As they conversed about the Bible, Bill asked one more logical question:

"Are you a Christian?"

The Uber driver responded a bit differently than you might think. He said, "No, I'm not a Christian. At least if you mean by *Christian* those who ride with me every day and tell me they are a Christian, but curse, get dropped off at the bars, or worse.... No, I am not a Christian! But I am a follower of Jesus."

Ouch.

Our behaviors matter. Our code matters.

Think about Abraham. He entered the promised land as a foreigner, a stranger. In Genesis 15, God gives Abraham a great vision. His descendants were going to be like the stars of heaven. I imagine that on every clear night Abraham must've wandered outside and taken great comfort that his family would be like that someday.

That vision is enough to guide Abraham's little family at the beginning. Abraham's family goes down to Egypt. For four hundred years, they are in slavery. By the time Abraham's family—led by Moses—returns to the promised land, they are no longer a little family. The Bible records in Exodus 38:26 that there are more than 600,000 men. As other historians note, if we include women and children, they are over a million strong.[12]

Now pause for a second. It's one thing to manage a little household like Abraham, Sarah, and Isaac. But it's entirely another thing to manage a million people.

What does God do?

He gives Moses the Ten Commandments. The first four commandments are upward commandments—how do we live and respond to a sovereign God? We love Him, we put Him first, we honor His name. The following six commandments teach us how we live in community with our fellow humans—we don't lie, cheat, steal, or murder.

In theory, those Ten Commandments might have been enough for the young nation to prosper, but alas, we are a broken people, so God also prescribed a set of rules, which we read in the books of Exodus, Leviticus, and Deuteronomy. Think of God as the very first legislator. God also prescribed a system of judges by which disputes among the people might be resolved.

Now I know that many people get lost in all the Old Testament laws, and it's hard to read through them. In fact, many a "read through the Bible in a year" program has stalled and been abandoned in the reading of the Law.

But we look at the laws incorrectly. The laws are really a code. At one level those laws were helpful to the nation of Israel. They taught them how to live in a new identity.

The laws also were helpful for a second big reason—they set Israel apart as a unique nation. Not only did their code reinforce their identity but it created curiosity. To the surrounding nations, Israel must have seemed one peculiar people. They didn't have a king; God was their king. They only had one God; in fact, they put Him right in the center of their camp. Then, at least one day a week, they stopped work, took a rest, and honored that same God. They were taught to love and respect one another and not just be a warring people. Strange indeed.

Here's the crazy part. As the family of Abraham multiplied and became the nation of Israel, they became an influence on the entire living world. Why were they such an influence? Because they lived differently. The other nations worshiped idols. If Israel followed its code, it would be the only nation with *one* God—and insisting only one God deserved the world's devotion.

Out of the seed of Abraham, God promised that there would one day come a Redeemer, one who would restore a broken world.

Admittedly that story is divisive because Jesus Himself declared that He was the *only* way to a right relationship with God. While that right relationship with God is easily obtained—faith in Jesus alone and the repentance of sin— that's where the trouble begins. Our world and our individual hearts chafe at the brave exclusivity of God. Who makes such bold assertions that they alone can save? Well, um, it's God who can make such blanket statements.

The law took the lofty idea that only one God brings salvation and turned it into practical, daily guidance for life. And the code, this way of living differently, stands out. A watching and waiting world looks at those who live differently and thinks, *I wonder if there really is a God.*

What a Code Is NOT

In all this talk of codes, we must remember one more truth: The Israelites failed to live by God's code. They failed miserably. Over and over, through the rest of the Old Testament, the Israelites kept abandoning God's code. The following books speak of affairs, revolts, murders, betrayals—and God's continued pleading with them to return.

The code informed their identity as God's people, but when they failed continually, they never lost their identity. Israel remained God's chosen people through whom He would send a Savior. The code served as a standard but never as transformation. Never as salvation.

> **The code served as a standard but never as transformation.**

The Israelites failed over and over, yet then came the redemption—God became human and entered the world.

Jesus, God's Son, lived by the code. Fully. Perfectly. He died as a perfect sacrifice for every one of us who never measure up to God's standards. None of us do. When we put our faith in Jesus as our only hope, He gives us a new identity.

Because we have a new identity, we also inherit a better way to live. The burden of measuring up has been removed. When we place our faith in Jesus, we receive His perfection. The code becomes a path of joy, a way of living out this new identity as God's chosen people.

Just as Israel was God's chosen nation and they could not lose their identity no matter how many times they failed, so now we as followers of Christ are God's chosen people and cannot lose our identity.

A code doesn't give us our identity. It only helps shape it.

So, let me encourage you: Write out your code. Review it. Remind yourself of it. Develop your family code. It's part of the legacy practice. And then we can take the next step toward living the Legacy Life—trusting that God can restore a fractured past.

7

REPAIRING *the* PAST

Forgiveness does not change the past, but it does enlarge the future.

Paul Boose

We'll take a turn here. The first two chapters of this section provide some very practical "chart your course" instruction. If you are going to live a Legacy Life, then you've got to have a map. You've got to have a plan. Or you'll certainly fail.

But there's something more. To lead a Legacy Life, you've got to repair your past.

When our kids were still in elementary school, during the summers we'd take off for two weeks. The dates were marked on the calendar, and everyone prepared with great anticipation.

Vacation meant loading up the station wagon with the right camping equipment—pans, metal cups, pocketknives, hats, bug spray, matches, hiking shorts, extra socks, and so on. Food was the most important. For the car ride, the snacks could bring peace, whether crackers or lollipops (to stop the chatter!) or the occasional candy bar. There was a cooler packed with ice for the things we'd need at the campsite—hot dogs, fixings for s'mores, and soft drinks.

We towed behind us one of those pop-up campers. So many times, we'd set out and go where the winds took us. We were just glad to be going somewhere. After hours of driving, we'd slide into a campground, set up our camper, start a campfire, and be good. Over those summers, we traveled through forty states or more.

> Only those who navigate the waters of conflict will succeed for generations to come.

While it was all great fun, there was something we didn't prepare for quite as well. If you've ever taken your kids on long car rides, you know where I'm going next. It's the inevitable cry from the back seat: "Are we there yet?" And even better, "Mom, he's on my side of the seat!" Or "He's looking at me funny!" Or "He touched me!"

Those little squabbles never got out of hand, but they inevitably joined us on the journey. They could break out into unpleasant scenes, hurt feelings, and threats from the front seat to the back. Some of it would last for miles, and some of it lasted until the next nap or the next campfire.

But that conflict was reality. Here's the truth of those who want to live the Legacy Life: Only those who navigate the waters of conflict will succeed for generations to come.

No Perfect Family

My biggest goal in navigating conflict has always been to foster an atmosphere of love. I want everyone to know that they are loved and welcome. Love is attractive and helps us weather our storms—even if we have difficult conversations. While my family and I are far from perfect when it comes to navigating conflict, when we turn to Scripture, we are hard-pressed to find the model family.

The world's not particularly old when the fall occurs. With the taste of apple in his mouth, instead of owning up, Adam blames Eve for the disaster. Like a schoolchild, he whines, "She gave it to me."

Flip a few pages forward. Cain kills his brother Abel. That's extreme family conflict.

Fast-forward to Abraham. He abandons his own son, Ishmael, because his wife is jealous.

Abraham's other son, Isaac, gives birth to two sweet little boys. Uh, not really. Esau and Jacob are born to tussle. Jacob steals the birthright from his brother and later deceives his father into giving him the blessing intended for his brother Esau. Esau plans a murder, so Jacob flees.

Jacob's flight leads him to the house of his uncle, Laban. A perfect place of refuge? Well, Laban makes Jacob work seven years only to literally switch the bride on the wedding night. Jacob's got to work another seven years to gain his true bride. Jacob and Laban continue to do battle like a labor union fight.

There's more. I'm quite sure that Abraham could never have imagined the ongoing conflict—and it sure wasn't mentioned in God's original promise. Jacob, now called Israel, has twelve sons, but he admittedly plays favorites. While the other brothers dress in the drab colors of the day, Joseph gets a coat of many colors. (I think that would make me mad too!) The other brothers do what any other family would do, right? They sell him into slavery. And they lie to cover it up.

But the drama doesn't stop there. It continues into the generations.

Miriam gossiped against her brother Moses. It cost her seven days of leprosy.

David's own son, Absalom, conspired to take the throne from his father.

By the time of Rehoboam, the families who started out as twelve tribes—one nation, one family—well, they split. The succeeding years are marked by periods of peace and war between them.

With these kinds of examples, we might ask whether there's hope for any family.

The Problem of Family Conflict

The problems with family conflict are not limited to biblical families, however. In the family business context, although the principles hold true for every family, the Truist Wealth Center for Family Legacy notes that a critical success factor is a conflict resolution policy, which "ensures that when disagreements arise in families there is a thoughtful, previously-determined protocol in place to resolve them efficiently, fairly and with minimal disruption to the family."[1]

The Pritzker family is but one family business example.[2]

Two brothers, Jay and Robert Pritzker, inherited the family business. Their grandfather had started a law firm, and their father had joined the firm, then began investing in real estate and businesses. He taught his sons to do the same. Jay demonstrated the same knack for deals that his father had, and by 1953, he bought his first company. Jay installed his brother Robert as the operator. That became their model. Jay would find a business to buy, and Robert would step in and turn it to profitability.

That model worked well—to the tune of two hundred businesses. The biggest of those became Hyatt Hotels, which became a multibillion-dollar holding in the Pritzker empire. As the business was growing, Jay had five children. Robert married later in life and had two children.

When Jay's oldest daughter was twenty-four years old, she committed suicide. Her death was never talked about among the Pritzker clan, but Jay mourned deeply. Jay funneled his energies into his second child, who joined the family business in 1978. His third and fourth children later joined the empire as well but never showed the same skill as their older brother.

Despite the varying skill levels, the Pritzker clan seemed to be happy enough—from the outside. They shared an 860-acre farm and investment opportunities. Indeed, Jay's number one goal was that his family remain unified. His hope was that his children would never let their financial wealth ruin them but instead focus on growing their collective wealth and be charitably focused.

He endeavored to provide each of his family members, including nieces and nephews, a comfortable lifestyle that would equate to $25 million per person over time.

Unfortunately, by 1997, Jay suffered a stroke, and the happy facade of the family began to crumble. After Jay's death in 1999, long-lying tensions came to light. Jay's children hatched a plan to exclude Robert's children, their cousins, from the family wealth. Robert himself raided the trusts of his own children and donated their shares to the family foundation. Robert's daughter then sued the family and ended up settling for millions of dollars.[3]

The Pritzker family mirrors the same kind of conflict that has occurred with so many families over time. The Vanderbilts, the Rockefellers, the Kochs, the Gores, the Goldmans, and others.[4]

The sensationalism among these stories may seem out of touch with everyday reality. But the truth is that these stories represent the same failed legacy.

Of conflicts not addressed—just avoided.

Of great intentions but poor follow-through.

Of children never allowed to develop.

Of the weight of the past.

Each of these stories speaks of horrible lessons in how not to do things. Yet they do not speak of how we might avoid their mistakes and do better in our own families. There are lessons to be learned from these situations. I'll be the first to admit that I have much to learn, and here is where some of Bill's experience in law practice and family consulting is most helpful.

Repairing the Past

No matter what you read into these words, the Pritzkers failed not because they had money, but because the money only highlighted problems that already existed.

Every family faces the same pitfalls. Jay Pritzker was like every father. He desperately wanted the unity of the family.

He wanted them to carry on with the same set of values: Work hard, contribute to the good of the world, don't seek your personal gain first, be charitable. On the other hand, if we use the Pritzkers as an example, we can see some of the failures.

- First and foremost, they avoided their conflict.
- The individual desires and greed triumphed over the commitment to the purpose of the family to have an impact on the world around them.
- Jay never fully addressed the aspirations of his two sons to do something other than the family business.
- They didn't talk about the hurts of the past—his daughter's suicide was a gaping hole in the family story.
- They allowed secrets, conspiracies, and factions to build instead of transparency.

There's a cycle of conflict that is the same in every family. It goes like this:

1. *Disruption.* There's a break in communication. That break may be as simple as a miscommunication or misunderstanding. It may be something stronger, like hurtful words that create an offense. That disruption is the first step, however.
2. *Broken trust.* That disruption leads to broken trust. There's hurt, pain, and a reluctance to share openly with the person who caused the hurt.

3. *Gossip and triangulation.* Instead of confronting the conflict head-on, the tendency is to go to another person in the family and triangulate the conversation. We might confuse the conversation as "seeking advice," but in reality, if we are involving another person who is not a solution to the disruption, we are only making it worse.
4. *Withdrawal, apathy, or separation.* When there's broken trust, gossip or triangulation may well lead to support for our feelings of distrust. As a result, the tendency is to withdraw—"I'm not going there again." Or it may be apathy—"I'm not having that conversation again." Or worse, separation—"I'm not going to engage at all."

Once there's withdrawal, apathy, or separation, the seeds are planted for ongoing, unresolved conflict. If they remain unresolved and unaddressed, then the seeds may give bloom to ongoing generational conflict.

A quick word about a trend that we've seen more often these days. We've had more and more families come up to us at our leadership events who say they find themselves in a situation where they are separated from their children. That separation may be the result of the parent's choosing or the child's.

Sometimes separation is necessary, particularly when safety is an issue. Sometimes separation is necessary because of addiction issues and the need to draw boundaries.

But overall, the goal—as much as it's possible—is to make separation a choice of last resort. The problem with separation is that it cuts off the family story, and if there are grandchildren involved, everyone must pretend that there's not a larger family. The reality is that your family will always be your family, and as long as there is a commitment to love one another, then the goal ought to be to lean in and work to make things better.

Cultivating an atmosphere of grace is essential for families. All of us are navigating this path of life for the first time.

What's the better way? The better way for navigating family conflict looks like this:

1. *Disruption.* There's an event, word, or incident that causes miscommunication, offense, or a break in relationship and creates disruption.
2. *Believe the best.* Instead of choosing gossip or triangulation, the first step is to believe the best about the situation, yourself, and the other person. We do not assume malice. We may experience bad behavior, but the root is not ill intent. This principle of believing the best is one of the first keys to successful conflict management.
3. *Engage.* Instead of avoiding the conflict, engage with the other person who created the disruption. Address it head-on. I'm not here to address all the methods of successful conflict management, but suffice it to say that there are countless books on the topic. The Scriptures are equally clear about the necessity of addressing conflict as a first priority.
4. *Seek understanding and restoration.* Our goal in conflict should be to understand the root cause—what

caused the disruption, but even more so to understand the nature of the offense and the impact that it caused. The goal is not punishment of the person who caused the harm. The goal is restoration of the relationship. The hallmark of this conversation is marked by statements like "I'm sorry" and "Will you forgive me?"

At the end of the day, this latter approach helps individuals and families maintain relationships today and for generations to come. The fundamental difference between the two approaches? One leads to withdrawal, apathy, or separation, while the other leads to restoration. It boils down to this:

Are you willing to fight for the relationship?
Are you willing to fight for the family?
Are you willing to fight for wholeness?

What If It Fails?

This advice on family conflict might seem a bit too Pollyanna for some. I'll be the first to admit, it's certainly the harder route. Can refusing to give up on a relationship really work? You might be thinking, "But you don't know my family," or "I can't believe the best; I know they meant to hurt me."

I don't want to be naive here. Each of us can only account for 50 percent of a relationship. The other 50 percent lies with the other party. And 50 percent is always a failing grade, unless the other person puts in effort as well.

What do we do when we try to engage with them and the conflict only gets worse? What happens when we seek restoration and receive further attacks? Romans 12:17–21 tells us how to respond in these situations:

> Do not repay anyone evil for evil. Be careful to do what is right in the eyes of everyone. If it is possible, as far as it depends on you, live at peace with everyone. Do not take revenge, my dear friends, but leave room for God's wrath, for it is written: "It is mine to avenge; I will repay," says the Lord. On the contrary:
>
>> "If your enemy is hungry, feed him;
>>   if he is thirsty, give him something to drink.
>> In doing this, you will heap burning coals on his
>>   head."
>
> Do not be overcome by evil, but overcome evil with good.

When a family member truly acts against us, we give up our right for revenge. We entrust the family member to God, and we follow God's command to love our enemies. We pray for those who persecute us. We never give up hope for a family member to have a change of heart, and we trust that God can change their heart of stone and give them a heart of flesh.

Preparing for Conflict

Admittedly, I tread lightly here. I believe our family has done a good job in transmitting our values, but it will be up to the succeeding generations to live it out. Let me say a word about the generations.

When the first generation is alive and present, they tend to be the convener of family meetings and family gatherings. They are the ones who call together the family for Christmas, Easter, the family reunion, the family vacation, or whatever the activity. The first generation serves in this role on a de facto basis. Generally, everyone looks to the first generation to set the lead. That leadership role is often just based upon positional authority. Sometimes I call this the "elephant in the room." It happens when you have the authority; you hold sway over everyone's decisions. This isn't ideal. The best thing, though hard, is to encourage others to become part of the process.

> As long as we are a broken people, we will have the need to repair our conflicts.

Once the first generation passes away, the next generation, usually siblings, must figure out how to work together. Their past experiences made them equals. None of them has positional authority over another, and they are forced to make decisions by committee. That committee approach is often difficult because committees make poor leaders, and, additionally, usually the loudest voice prevails.

Within this generational discussion is the essential need to repair the past. We must commit to resolve past and present disputes. That need will be present in every generation. And believe me, I need to remember this message as much as the next person. As long as we are a broken people, we will have the need to repair our conflicts.

There's a critical scene in the New Testament. The gospel is advancing rapidly, and the church is expanding well beyond Jerusalem. The apostle Paul and Barnabas are at the forefront of this rapid expansion. As they get ready to head out on their second missionary journey, Barnabas wants to take John Mark with him. Paul refuses. John Mark had abandoned them on a previous journey.

This is no small tussle. The Scriptures record it as a "sharp disagreement" (Acts 15:39). It's so sharp that Barnabas splits from Paul; he takes John Mark with him, and Paul takes Silas. Here's the critical point. Paul, Barnabas, John Mark, and Silas did not withdraw. They did not retreat into apathy. They might well have taken the approach, "Aw, it's the church again, too much fighting, so I'm going to sit on the sidelines." I'm afraid our churches and families are like that—people sitting on the sidelines because of past hurts.

I'm so glad that these leaders did not pull away but remained engaged. There was too much at stake: the advance of the gospel to a watching and waiting world. How we manage our conflicts speaks volumes to a very lost world searching for answers. As a final postscript, we know that while Paul and John Mark had conflict in the moment, by the end of Paul's life, he describes John Mark as "helpful" to him (2 Tim. 4:11).

Allow for Grace

As I write, I realize there are some who will find these pages difficult. They may find themselves in a place where relationships are strained, estranged, or even irreparable. They may likewise be in a place where their children have chosen very different lifestyles and values—even values that are polar opposite to the ones in which they were raised. To the extent they gather as a family, their gatherings may seem bland

and lacking depth, and they are careful to avoid too many subjects in the name of keeping the peace.

Bill tells me when he leads his workshops that those families with adult children come up to him with a simple question: "Where were you twenty-five years ago when I needed you?" They despair. How do you put the toothpaste back into the tube?

Sometimes the issues rest with the parents themselves, whether from the end of a marriage or a life spent at work away from family. How do you talk about legacy in the midst of these circumstances? How do you talk about legacy when all seems broken? For much of our lives, God gives us circumstances that seem a mystery. We face life situations that just don't make sense.

But God always has a way of redeeming and turning the story around in ways that we cannot see or imagine.

Throughout the Scriptures, we see time and again that God works through the broken. He can raise up a shepherd boy to be a king. He can make a teenage virgin the mother of the Messiah. He can take the man most opposed to Christ, Paul, and turn him into His missionary to leaders and kings of the world.

So, take heart. Our God is a God of grace. He thinks in terms of generations. It is not the right now and the right here that we live for. It is not even just how our children or grandchildren are doing. Pray for the generations of your family. Pray that God will restore the foundations and that He will restore your family. Do your part. Apologize. Seek to mend what was ripped. Forgive. Keep an atmosphere of love. And keep praying.

No matter what, don't give up. Whatever may seem amiss now, God will correct and set aright in the generations to come. Even though the legacy may seem broken, God will restore and redeem it. What once lay in ruins will one day turn into a story of grace.

8

SHARING YOUR STORY

Your story is the greatest legacy that you will leave to your friends. It's the longest-lasting legacy you will leave to your heirs.

Steve Saint

For more than twenty years, Bill and I have been working together. We host leaders from around the country. It's been a unique time. We've heard from so many of those leaders about how that time has impacted their lives. Some have told us powerfully how they've redirected their giving, sold businesses, given up ownership, reunited with family, and even prayed to receive Christ.

But we don't have sermons.

Or breakout sessions.

Or teaching outlines.

Or neat three-point applications.

We share stories.

I tell them the story of my growing-up years, of picking cotton, of small churches, and of equally small offerings. We moved from town to town. I switched schools twelve or thirteen times over those years. As I said earlier, by high school, I was leaving school by 10:30 a.m. through a Distributive Education program and going to work at the local five-and-dime. That gave wings to my retail career, first at TG&Y, then later as I started our little business in the garage. Our failures got mixed in along with our adventures of faith. We eventually turned to our journey of generosity and wrestling with God's ownership.

The funny thing is that I've told that same story hundreds of times now. No matter how many times I tell it, it never gets old. People still keep coming to hear.

For me, there are still moments when telling that story that I'll choke up, tears will come to my eyes, and I'll remember how it felt. It still moves me, for instance, to tell the story of my mother upon her deathbed as the angels came to take her home. When I describe the struggle of the Supreme Court case, I can feel the worry of that court case and later the calm that came over me. I'll also use the time to share some humor, and because Bill is a lawyer, I get to tell all kinds of lawyer jokes—and there are lots of them!

> **When we share our stories, we bear witness to the work of God in our lives. We testify to the fact that we are not alone, that God goes before us.**

Why does the story remain fresh and new? Why does each retelling bring something unique? Revelation 12:11 says,

"They triumphed over him by the blood of the Lamb and by the *word of their testimony*." When we share our stories, we bear witness to the work of God in our lives. We testify to the fact that we are not alone, that God goes before us, and that we are dependent on Him. God uses that witness to give us victory!

What About These Stones?

There are a lot of stones and altars in the Bible.

> Noah built an altar of stones after the flood (Gen. 8:20).
> Abraham built an altar of stones after entering the promised land (Gen. 12:7).
> On two different occasions, Isaac and then Jacob built altars of stone after God appeared to them in a dream (Gen. 26:25; 28:18).
> Moses built an altar of stones and called the place "The LORD is my banner" (Exod. 17:15).
> When the Israelites crossed into the promised land, they set up a pile of stones as a memorial (Josh. 4:8–9, 21–24).
> Samuel, after a victorious battle over the Philistines, set up a stone of remembrance that he called Ebenezer (1 Sam. 7:12).

These are just a few examples. Why these stones? The stones were a physical reminder of a spiritual truth. The stones are a reminder of the presence of God and His faithfulness.

Think about it; how many times might a parent pass by those stones and use them as a visual reminder of God's care for their children? In Joshua 4:21–22, Joshua illustrates the point, saying to the Israelites, "In the future when your descendants ask their parents, 'What do these stones mean?' tell them, 'Israel crossed the Jordan on dry ground.'"

While I'm not advocating that you go build an altar or stack a pile of stones somewhere, the instruction from the Scriptures is to pay attention to those God-moments. Whenever you have one of those moments, preserve it and take time to tell that story at your dinner table.

Even set up a physical reminder of God's faithfulness.

For my family, one of our stones is the frame chopper that Larry Pico and I bought to start the framing business that grew into Hobby Lobby. The green metal chopper stands about three feet tall, and we have it on display still today in Hobby Lobby's headquarters, just down a hallway from my office. Above the chopper hangs a framed copy of one of the pages from our first sales flier from 1970—nine hand-drawn images of our frames for sale and their prices. When Bill and I host leaders' conferences, we walk groups down the hallways and circle them around the chopper. Sure, I could tell the same story from the conference room—but there's something about standing in front of the tangible items that makes the story stick.

The group stands in front of the display, and I tell them about the small investment of six hundred dollars that felt so big and risky at the time. I tell of Barbara's hard work, how she really started the business. How our sons chipped in gluing frames together, and how we paid them seven cents per frame. How we depended on each other as a family, and how God faithfully sustained us.

I keep that chopper displayed in our headquarters because it reminds me where we started and just how much God has done since then. And it gives me a reason to tell the story. Over and over.

The Power of Story

The power of the stones rests in a simple concept. The stones represent a physical place. They represent a moment in time. With that geographic moment, there's literally a physical reaction. Jennifer Allen Craft defines *place* like this: "Places are the ground of shared human experience as well as the product of shared human experience."[1]

I like to keep things simple, so let me say it like this: Every one of us has a list of places that are important to us. It might include places like these:

- the old family home where we were raised
- the elementary school where we squared off with a bully
- the church or physical place where we received Christ
- the spot where we proposed to our spouse
- the place where we got fired or got a promotion
- the place of our greatest triumph
- the place where we hit rock bottom

For me, two places stand out: One is my office, specifically the underside of my wooden desk. In 1985, when Hobby Lobby couldn't pay its bills, I thought we would shut down. I closed the door of my office, crawled under my desk, and cried out to God. I knew I had started trying to run the business on my own strength, thinking I didn't need Him, and He had to humble me. Those prayers marked a turning point, and the company slowly turned around and recovered.

The second place is my backyard. One evening in the late 1990s, I felt particularly overwhelmed by the weight of the company and what it would mean if it were passed on to my family. I had followed the advice of our lawyers and accountants, but I just didn't feel right about how we had set up the ownership structure. I walked out to the backyard to pray, and there God spoke to me that He owned the company, not me. I went back inside and wrote down on a slip of paper, "I own Hobby Lobby. Signed, God." From that moment, I worked with our lawyers to restructure Hobby Lobby's ownership to reflect that the company belongs to God, not us. I still keep that slip of paper as a reminder of this truth.

Now think about your places. You probably have your own list of places that have extra-special meaning for you. I'm guessing that you didn't make a pile of rocks or build an altar and offer a sacrifice. But your places are tied to their own unique stories.

Take a few moments and write down some of the significant places in your life and what you remember about those places. For each place, take a moment to write down the lesson or meaning of the place.

That's the idea of these memorial piles of rocks. The stones tell us that something important happened. They also tell us that there is an underlying story. (One quick digression: Bill's ministry is built around the idea of these stones; his ministry is called Legacy Stone.)

The Power of Repetition

Our job is to tell and retell that story. Because within the story, there's emotion. By retelling that story, we relive and remember what happened.

God's desire is that we retell that story. Is it any wonder that God designed seven festivals to take place each year? Chief among those festivals was Passover. This festival commemorated how God delivered His people out of slavery and how He spared them from death.

Passover begins with a story. Exodus 12:26–27 says, "And when your children ask you, 'What does this ceremony mean to you?' then tell them, 'It is the Passover sacrifice to the LORD.'" God created an entire holiday just to give parents a chance to tell the story. The Passover and this concept of remembering are repeated in the Psalms: "I will remember the deeds of the LORD; yes, I will remember your miracles of long ago. . . . You led your people like a flock by the hand of Moses and Aaron" (77:11, 20). Even though more than four hundred years have passed from the time of the first Passover, the writers of the Psalms are still encouraging Israel to remember how God delivered them.[2]

More than just Passover encouraged the Israelites to remember God's story. Six other festivals all carried the same idea. In general, each of the festivals were marked by pulling away from work and setting aside time to fellowship and to remember what God had done for His people.

We should not forget that God also established a weekly festival—the Sabbath. The Sabbath incorporated the same concepts: Rest from work. Reflection. And fellowship.

If you fast-forward to the New Testament, you see the same idea. Jesus taught in parables. His disciples questioned Him about why He used stories, and Jesus replied, "You've been given insight into God's kingdom. You know how it works. Not everybody has this gift, this insight; it hasn't been given to them. . . . That's why I tell stories: to create readiness, to nudge the people toward a welcome awakening" (Matt. 13:11–15 MSG).

Jesus knew that stories would most powerfully convey truth.

So, let's come full circle. We started this chapter talking about the events that Bill and I lead each year. We've been sharing the same story again and again. It doesn't get old, because I get to revisit the work of God in my life and our family's life. From our story, others learn how they may be like us or different from us, but they get an opportunity to apply it to their own story.

Stories Preserve Families and Culture

Storytelling is not just a biblical concept. There's an old proverb whose origin is hard to discern, but it goes like this: Those who tell the stories rule the world.

Here are a few other quotes that illustrate the prevalence of story throughout history:

"Great stories happen to those who can tell them."
—Ira Glass[3]

"Our species thinks in metaphors and learns through stories."—Mary Catherine Bateson[4]

"Where there is an absence of story, or perhaps a bad story, a good storyteller walks in and changes reality."—Donald Miller[5]

National Geographic published an article about storytelling that offered this insight: "Before there was writing, there was storytelling. It occurs in every culture and from every age. It exists (and existed) to entertain, to inform, and to promulgate cultural traditions and values."[6]

That article points out different cultures around the world that use storytelling to preserve their values and culture. In referencing Hawaiian culture, the article notes that storytellers were honored members of society: "Hawaiians valued the stories because they were not only entertaining, but they also taught the next generation about behavior, values, and traditions."[7]

> **Storytelling takes time. And if we don't make time—intentional time—we lose our culture and the soul of who we are.**

Let me pause with a word of caution. In our Western world, we live such busy lives, floating from activity to activity. Storytelling takes time. And if we don't make time—intentional time—we lose our culture and the soul of who we are and who we are meant to be.

But there's another warning as well. In our television-, movie-, and social media–driven world, we tend to be watchers of stories. The stories are created for us. We are passive in our story. It's only those who actively work to preserve and tell their stories who succeed.

When my kids were young, making time for stories looked like taking trips as a family. We went on road trips around the US. During the long car rides, we filled the time with stories of our parents and grandparents and their service to the Lord. Now that my children are adults with families and grandchildren of their own, we still take time to gather. We gather monthly to discuss our giving, quarterly to celebrate birthdays, and annually to celebrate our vision, mission, and values. With grandchildren and great-grandchildren with different pursuits, we do our best to gather everyone. During these times, we remind each other of the stories of God's work in our family.

What Are Your Top-Ten Stories?

If you want to live a life that has generational impact, if you want to have a family that thrives for generations, storytelling is one of the first keys. James Hughes says that family stories "are the glue that binds together the individual members of the family. Family stories give members a sense of the unique history and values they share, their 'differentness.'"[8]

But to tell your stories, you must know what they are. When I speak to groups, I tell them my life is focused on seven or eight pivotal events. Those events are at the heart of the stories I tell. Some of them are great stories. For instance, I can tell

- about the time when God nudged me to give $30,000 when I didn't have it, which helped reveal my calling as a merchant;

- about when God challenged us to outgive Him—we didn't know how, but we tried—and it's led us on a great journey of generosity;
- about when God nudged us to close on Sundays even though that day was our most profitable day per hour.

Some of the stories come from the wilderness, like

- when we needed a word from God during the first dark days of the COVID-19 pandemic, and He gave us three phrases—He'd guide us, He'd guard us, and He'd groom us;
- when God comforted us through the prayers of others and gave us a sense of calm during the Supreme Court case;
- when we had to wrestle with the weight of the company we'd built and whether we truly considered God the owner of our business.

When Bill leads one of his family legacy workshops, he'll ask a question to the families participating: What are the top-ten stories your family needs to know?

That part of the workshop is one of the most fun for the participants because they can reflect on their own journey. Most families come up with far more than ten stories to share, but they all have the same common themes.

Usually, there was a moment of brokenness where God met them, a moment of personal faith when God became more real to them, and a story around a struggle with business and career where God redirected them.

The stories are a mixture of joy and loss, or sometimes they're just fun. Do you want to live a Legacy Life? Do you want to set in motion a powerful legacy? Then you'll be one of those who take care to preserve their story.

Let me offer a warning as well. If you don't take care of your story, no one else will. There's a saying I've heard many different ways, but it goes like this: When a person dies, a library burns.

Only you can save the library. Take this encouragement, pause reading, and write down your top-ten stories—at least the bullet points of the stories you want to tell.

What About the "Bad" Stories?

Sometimes in listing stories, people will ask, "What if my story is a bad one?" We understand this question. Not every life story feels like a heartwarming tale to tell the grandkids.

When Bill and I do our events, we'll joke about who was the poorest growing up. Now, I grew up during the 1940s, and back then it seemed everyone was poor, but we were definitely taking it to the extreme. Back in those days, you'd have ice delivered to your house. That ice was used to keep things cold in the refrigerator, which was appropriately called the icebox. When the ice delivery man came to bring ice to us, we were embarrassed by the fact that we didn't have any food in the icebox. So we'd cover it up. We'd place empty bowls in the refrigerator and cover them with plates so the ice man wouldn't know that we didn't have anything.

Bill has his own stories. He was named after his great-grandfather who was a moonshiner. His grandfather raised eight children in a three-room log cabin in the hills of the Missouri Ozarks. By all accounts, his grandfather was not described as a nice man. Bill's dad came from that line. In addition, Bill's dad was an alcoholic, and with a few beers in him, he became abusive with his words and sometimes with his belt. A lifelong smoker, Bill's dad got lung cancer, and in the final months of his life, the family was left largely destitute. Sometimes there was nothing in the refrigerator other than a bowl of beans.

When Bill's father died, they were literally weeks away from becoming homeless. His dad died without life insurance, a pension, or any assets. His mom did not work outside the home and did not have a driver's license. They could have landed on the streets if not for God's intervention.

What do you do with these difficult stories? We know that there are stories far more difficult than our own. Maya Angelou writes, "There is no greater agony than bearing an untold story inside you."[9] Sometimes in sharing our stories we find healing.

How do you find redemption in family stories that are seemingly unredeemable?

Let's return to the family story of Abraham. When most people think of Abraham, they think of Genesis 12. There, God gives Abraham a promise of land, blessing, and reputation. When we read the words of Genesis 12, we applaud Abraham for being such a great example of faith.

But Abraham's story actually starts in Genesis 11. It's a small prologue in the story:

This is the account of Terah's family line.

Terah became the father of Abram, Nahor and Haran. And Haran became the father of Lot. . . . Abram and Nahor both married. The name of Abram's wife was Sarai. . . . Now Sarai was childless because she was not able to conceive.

Terah took his son Abram, his grandson Lot son of Haran, and his daughter-in-law Sarai, the wife of his son Abram, and together they set out from Ur of the Chaldeans to go to Canaan. But when they came to Harran, they settled there. (vv. 27–31)

What do we learn about Abraham's family?

This short little narrative speaks volumes. We know from later Scriptures that Terah is an idolater.[10] Sarah is barren. Back then, a woman's ability to conceive, particularly a son, was a central point of her identity. Her inability to conceive tells us there's pain in this family's story. Terah sets out to leave his homeland. Two of his sons, Haran and Nahor, do not come with him. Haran has died, but what about Nahor? The text gives us no clue as to why Nahor does not leave with them. We are left to wonder—did he die? Was there family conflict? Was he comfortable in his current environment? Only Abraham and Lot go with Terah.

Then, despite the vision of going to Canaan, the small cluster of travelers stops short. They never get there. They settle for the land of Harran when they could have continued to the promised land. The absence of these details tells us there's a lot going on in these few verses. Abraham's family is no perfect family.

With this backdrop, we get to Genesis 12, where God gives Abraham the very specific instruction to "Go from your country, your people and your father's household to the land I will show you" (Gen. 12:1). Abraham is to leave behind his country, a land of idol worshipers. He's to leave behind the larger household and his immediate family. He's to set out to be part of God's story in a new land with a new promise.

Here's the simple truth of these two passages: Our family history informs us, but only God defines us. He gives us our identity.

Abraham came from a family of idol worshipers. There's no apparent unity of calling—not everyone goes with Terah. Abraham doesn't even have a son; his lineage cannot continue. In looking at his father, Terah, well, we see that Terah settles. He stops short of the vision. All these things give information to Abraham about his past, but they do not limit his future.

Indeed, by Genesis 12, God is giving Abraham a new story, a new vision, and a new name. In Abraham's story, He'll bless the nations—no matter his troubled past.

Take heart from one of the founders of our faith. His story was not perfect. But Abraham didn't let it define him. Abraham let God define him and give him a brand-new identity. God can do the same with every one of our stories.

Pay attention to the story God has given you but remember He can give a new story for your future. That is truly the adventure of the life of faith. It is why we call it the legacy adventure.

We keep our vision for the future alive through the stories of others who have already lived out this adventure ahead of us.

PART 3
LEGACY ADVENTURES

9

THRIVING FAMILY LEGACIES *of the* BIBLE

Know therefore that the Lord your God is God; he is the faithful God, keeping his covenant of love to a thousand generations.

Deuteronomy 7:9

As you arrive here at this chapter, my hope is that you come with a renewed sense of hope. Everyone wants to live the Legacy Life, but we are plagued by short-term thinking. That short-term thinking flies in the face of God's desire for our lives and our families to impact the generations. How did we arrive at such a narrow view of our purpose? We accepted a worldview that values the individual over community, over family.

In part 2, "Legacy Practices," we've given you some practical steps to living the Legacy Life. First, chart your course with a generational vision, mission, and values statement. How do you live out your vision, mission, and values? You do that with a code of conduct, a way of life, and practical rhythms. As part of that process, you need to repair the past—be committed to addressing conflict while recognizing that grace is required. And finally, you need to own and tell your stories from generation to generation.

Here in part 3, we take on "Legacy Adventures." What do we mean by this? In this section, our goal is to give you some real-life stories, from the Bible and from history, of those families who live out generational legacy and also some of those who fail. In this chapter, we'll address a few of those legacy stories from the pages of Scripture, starting with the Rekabites.

The Rekabites

It's a little-noticed passage in Scripture, yet, as it turns out, it is the foundation for one of the greatest legacy stories in the Bible. The passage of 2 Kings 10:15–17 tells the story like this:

> After [Jehu] left there, he came upon Jehonadab son of Rekab, who was on his way to meet him. Jehu greeted him and said, "Are you in accord with me, as I am with you?"
>
> "I am," Jehonadab answered.
>
> "If so," said Jehu, "give me your hand." So he did, and Jehu helped him up into the chariot. Jehu said, "Come with me and see my zeal for the LORD." Then he had him ride along in his chariot.
>
> When Jehu came to Samaria, he killed all who were left there of Ahab's family; he destroyed them, according to the word of the LORD spoken to Elijah.

It's an unremarkable passage. You have to dig a bit more. King Ahab had been king of Israel, and he was one of the worst kings in Israel. In fact, 1 Kings 16:30 gives Ahab all-star evil status, saying he "did evil in the sight of the LORD, more than all who were before him" (ESV).

As kings are inclined to do in order to preserve their own legacy, Ahab had seventy sons. His reign of evil could last for a long time with that number of kids.

It's at this intersection that 2 Kings 10 occurs. Jehu is anointed by the prophet Elisha's understudy to be the next king. Part of his assignment is to wipe out the seventy sons of Ahab and to destroy the prophets of Baal. While he's on mission, Jehu encounters Jehonadab son of Rekab and asks a simple question: "Are you with me?" Jehonadab willingly joins the mission, and off the two warriors go to eradicate the evil from the land.

And that's it. That's all you hear of the story.

This is the high point of Jehu's career. He ascends to the throne, and whether he's a good or bad king is debatable. Further, there's no more mention of Jehonadab son of Rekab—at least in the book of Kings.

You actually have to turn to the book of Jeremiah before the story resumes. Jeremiah started his ministry as a youth (Jer. 1:6). For decades, he prophesies about the destruction of Israel if the people continue their faithless ways.

I suspect Jeremiah becomes weary—tired of preaching the same message. And he wonders, "Is there anybody still faithful?"

So in Jeremiah 35, God tells Jeremiah to bring in the Rekabites. Ding! Ding! Remember 2 Kings 10? Remember

Jehonadab? These are God's simple instructions to Jeremiah: Set before the Rekabites wine to drink.

I can almost imagine the Rekabites marching in a single file, sitting down in wonderment. "Why is the most renowned prophet of the day calling the Rekabites in for afternoon tea?"

But it's not tea. It's wine. And the Rekabites respond, incredulous: "Uh, we don't drink wine!" The Scriptures record their real response: "We do not drink wine, because our forefather Jehonadab son of Rekab gave us this command: 'Neither you nor your descendants *must ever* drink wine'" (Jer. 35:6).

In fact, Jehonadab gave more instructions to his kids (Jer. 35:5–8). Not only did he not want them to drink wine, but he also said:

Don't build houses.
Don't be farmers.
Don't plant vineyards.
Instead, live in tents.
Be nomads.

Now, I'm not sure what all the reasons were for Jehonadab's commands. I suspect he was wanting his children to stay away from the city and live the simple and pure life of the country where they'd have to depend on God for their needs.

But here's the punch line. Are you ready for this? How long had the Rekabites been faithful to obey the command of their ancestor?

For 250 years.[1]

Okay, I know we don't have all the exact timelines, but give or take, there were some 250 years that had passed from 2 Kings 10 to Jeremiah 35. Can you imagine 250 years of one family's legacy?

But it gets better.

We know that when Israel returns from captivity during the time of Nehemiah, there are Rekabites rebuilding the wall of Jerusalem—four hundred years after 2 Kings 10.[2]

It gets better still.

At the end of Jeremiah 35, God makes one of the most astounding promises in all of Scripture. He tells the Rekabites that because they've been faithful in obeying the voice of their father Jehonadab, they "shall never lack a man to stand before me" (v. 19 ESV). Wow, what a promise!

Ellicott's Commentary tells us that

- the Jewish historian Hegesippus recorded Rekabites present at the martyrdom of James and looking on in sympathy;
- in the twelfth century, Benjamin of Tudela tells of 100,000 Rekabites who lived near El Jubar;
- Signor Pierotti came across a band of Rekabites as late as 1862 near Mecca on the Dead Sea.[3]

Think about it: some two thousand years of one family carrying out their vision, mission, and values. That's success. That's family legacy. What we are talking about *is* possible through the power of God's Spirit working in you and your family. You have no idea what God can accomplish through your legacy if you are faithful.

Ezra and Phinehas

Have you ever read Ezra 7:10? You may have even heard sermons on this passage. It's a famous verse: "For Ezra had devoted himself to the study and observance of the Law of the LORD, and to teaching its decrees and laws in Israel."

It makes a nice three-point sermon. He studied. He observed. He taught. When you read that verse, you might think, "Way to go, Ezra! You are a good guy, a strong role model. That's what I want to do."

Hold that thought.

If we read Ezra 7:10 only in the context of how good Ezra was—the studying, the observing, the teaching—we miss the full impact of the story.

We have to read the verses beforehand for the legacy story. Here it is:

> After these things, during the reign of Artaxerxes king of Persia, Ezra son of Seraiah, the son of Azariah, the son of Hilkiah, the son of Shallum, the son of Zadok, the son of Ahitub, the son of Amariah, the son of Azariah, the son of Meraioth, the son of Zerahiah, the son of Uzzi, the son of Bukki, the son of Abishua, the son of Phinehas, the son of Eleazar, the son of Aaron the chief priest—*this Ezra* came up from Babylon. (Ezra 7:1–6)

If you're like me, you read these verses and your eyes glossed over. It's a bunch of names, and if you've ever tried to read the Bible through in a year, you skip this passage.

But stick with me. Let's do a bit of discovering.

I'd like you to flip over to Psalm 106:30–31. There, David is recounting the work of God back in the days of Egypt.

There's a worthy sidenote here. It's been five hundred years or more since God delivered Israel from Egypt. But David is still reflecting on God's work. (Hmm, I wonder if there's a lesson there . . . about remembering, not forgetting.)

In Psalm 106, as David is reflecting on God's work over the generations, at verse 30 and 31 he includes a curious interjection:

> But Phinehas stood up and intervened,
>   and the plague was checked.
> This was credited to him as righteousness
>   for endless generations to come.

Wait a minute. Phinehas was listed as one of Ezra's ancestors. Ezra to Phinehas? What's the connection?

First, take a look at Phinehas. He stood up and intervened. The plague was checked. The reference is to Numbers 25, where Israel is in the dark days of the wilderness. They are tired of manna. They are tired of the fresh meat that God has been providing day by day. They've lost sight of the vision, the promised land, the promise to Abraham. They've lost sight of the stars.

When you get weary of the vision, you look to satisfy your desires. And that's just what Israel does. They go out and hang out with foreign women. They engage in improper relationships. They worship the gods of these women. They become like the world. They lose sight of the fact that they are the children of Abraham called to a divine purpose.

As Moses, Aaron, and the leaders are grieving this betrayal of God, an Israelite man incredibly, brazenly, brings one of the Moabite women into the camp. In front of everyone.

He brings her into his tent. With the rest of his family. It's a classic "I don't care what anyone else says; I'm going to live my life how I want and satisfy my own desires because I don't care about what God has for us."

Everyone's stunned. Except Phinehas. He's probably a teen, but he rises up with righteous anger. He can't believe that this man would trample on the holiness of God. He kills them. And the plague is stopped.

Okay, pause. I'm not advocating murder, and I don't fully understand the cultural context of all that is happening here, but I know that for the times, this was a cultural turning point. And we must ask ourselves, How do we respond when the name and character of God are being defamed?

Back to Phinehas. God calls out Phinehas. He commends him for his zealous defense of God's name. Then, in a mic-drop moment, God makes a profound—even stunning—promise to Phinehas: "Behold, I give to him my covenant of peace, and it shall be to him and to his descendants after him the covenant of a perpetual priesthood, because he was jealous for his God and made atonement for the people of Israel" (Num. 25:12–13 ESV).

A covenant of peace.

For generations.

A perpetual priesthood.

Let the power of those words sink in—a generational promise to Phinehas. Sign me up for that!

Now we can turn back to Ezra 7:10. We discover the wonderful, beautiful point of this passage. Ezra 7:1–6 is the fulfillment of the age-old promise to Phinehas: "Ezra son of Seraiah . . . the son of Phinehas . . . this Ezra came up from Babylon." It's the covenant of peace. The perpetual priesthood. Ezra 7 represents fifteen generations from Phinehas. So it is with verse 6 that the writer points out *"this Ezra."* Ezra is part of the promise to Phinehas.

Oh, and here's the fun part. From Phinehas to Ezra? Some nine hundred years.[4]

Are you ready for one more?

The Perez Story

Don't you love the book of Ruth? It's such a heartwarming story. Here's a quick recap. There's a famine in Israel—Bethlehem in particular. That famine causes Elimilek and Naomi and their two sons to leave Bethlehem and settle in Moab.

Spoiler alert: If you remember from Numbers 25, bad things happen when you leave the vision of the promised land and go hang out in Moab. But the Scriptures are silent about all the circumstances, what's happening in Bethlehem and if Moab is really any better. But this we know:

Naomi's husband Elimilek dies. Sad.

Naomi's two sons marry two Moabite women, Orpah and Ruth. Happy, we think . . .

But then Naomi's two sons die. Sad again.

Even worse, Naomi is a widow in a foreign land. Without a husband, without her sons, she has no means of support. She's at the mercy of the welfare system, which is really just the good intentions of her neighbors. But she's a foreigner.

So Naomi returns to Bethlehem, her homeland, where she's got neighbors who may help her. She tells her daughters-in-law to stay in Moab and return to their families. It just makes sense. Naomi can't care for them. She's got no means of support. But Ruth pleads with Naomi, and in a famous passage of Scripture, she says, "Where you go I will go, and where you stay I will stay. Your people will be my people and your God my God" (Ruth 1:16).

I believe Ruth catches the vision of Naomi's life. The family of Israel—they are God's chosen people, and she wants to be part of that story!

Fast-forward. I won't go through all the details, but Ruth meets Boaz. Boaz is a good guy. He's called a "man of standing" (Ruth 2:1). He's a man of integrity. People know him at the city gates. His word and advice can be trusted.

Most readers focus on the love story, but this is where the story turns generational. When Ruth and Boaz get married, the elders of the town and the people gather at the city gates to bless them. Here's the blessing: "May the LORD make the woman who is coming into your home like Rachel and Leah, who together built up the family of Israel. May you have standing in Ephrathah and be famous in Bethlehem. Through the offspring the LORD gives you by this young woman, may your family be like that of Perez, whom Tamar bore to Judah" (Ruth 4:11–12).

A blessing of standing.

A blessing of fame—reputation.

A blessing to be like Perez.

Now, here we get curious. Who is Perez? Who is Tamar? You've got to turn all the way back to Genesis 38—some seven hundred years earlier.[5]

Judah, the fourth son of Jacob, gets married and has three sons. His first son, Er, marries Tamar. At this point, the story turns a bit weird, and we could get lost in those issues. They are a mix of cultural issues, familial responsibility, and family identity. Suffice it to say that Er dies, so does his brother, and Tamar is left a widow with no future prospect of a husband.

In that day, a widow—let alone a daughter-in-law—was in a precarious financial position. She's fully dependent on her father-in-law Judah for support.

A desperate Tamar literally hatches a plot to conceive and bear a child for her future well-being. She disguises herself as a prostitute, puts herself in Judah's path, and out of this illicit relationship she becomes pregnant. Ultimately, the child born of this very strange relationship is Perez.

Perez means "breakthrough." And while we must use our imagination here, it seems that Tamar and Perez decided to break away from their twisted path. They set a course for integrity and faith. In the fourth generation of Perez, Nahshon is a recognized leader, a prince of the tribe of Judah. Nahshon is the first to bring in his offering to the dedication of the altar (Num. 7:12–17). In Jewish tradition, as Pharaoh is pursuing Israel, Nahshon is considered to be the first to step into the sea as an act of faith before God parts the waters.[6]

> **They decided to break away from their twisted path. They set a course for integrity and faith.**

Nahshon's son, Salmon, marries Rahab from Jericho (Matt. 1:5). Rahab is mentioned in the Hall of Fame of faith in Hebrews 11. Some have speculated that Salmon was one of the spies that Rahab hid as Israel was getting ready to enter the promised land.[7]

Salmon's son is Boaz, and as we mentioned before, he's a "man of standing" in Bethlehem (Ruth 2:1). The commentators tell us that Boaz was quite likely a man of valor who had proven himself in battle.[8] The line of Boaz continues from Obed to Jesse to David. And the Davidic line leads, of course, to Jesus.

A few other notes about this line of Perez and Boaz: By 1 Chronicles 27:2–3, Jashobeam, a son of Perez, serves as a captain in David's army. Later still, as Israel returns from captivity in Babylon, there are 468 sons of Perez who are once again described as "men of standing" (Neh. 11:6).

Do you see the theme? Perez set in motion a life of integrity, a noble life, a life of valor, a Legacy Life. From Perez to the book of Nehemiah? Some 1,400 years.[9]

Lessons from These Biblical Stories

As we take a look at these legacy families from the Bible, they give us hope from the seemingly endless cycle of success and failure in the Scriptures. We see the roller coaster of faith particularly in the periods of the judges and the kings. For a time, Israel is faithful. Reform gets instituted. Then the next cycle follows. Sometimes it's lazy faith, the inability to decide that God is truly the one true God. Sometimes it's the disregard of God and the embracing of false gods. But in these three family stories we see several themes.

First, you see a fundamental zeal for God. Phinehas illustrates his passion for the holiness of God, to the point that he'll actively defend God's name.

Second, you can presume storytelling. When I think of the Rekabites, for instance, I think of a family gathered around the campfire night after night. There were probably three or four generations of them gathered.

In the absence of a Dr. Seuss reader, the youngest child was probably conditioned to ask for a story from the eldest Rekabite. And thus would commence Jehonadab or his descendants retelling the privilege of fighting alongside King Jehu. The wild ride in the chariot. The wind in his hair. The victory over evil. Restored order to the land. The uncertain end of Jehu. All of this followed by the call to stay sober, live in tents, be nomads, and be warriors, and then finished with the singular chant: "For we are Rekabites!" I imagine the lines of Phinehas and Perez were filled with similar stories.

Third, the call to vision. I can see it in each of these families. The Rekabites had a different vision for their family. They would live apart from others with a different life of faith and the promise from God that they would always have a man to stand before God. I think they repeated and reinforced that vision to the generations. The line of Phinehas marked a similar vision—an enduring priesthood, a covenant of peace from generation to generation. Ezra could trace his lineage back to that vision. In the same way, I think Perez echoed a similar vision, a breakthrough, a breakaway from the twisted foundations of his family to a new life of valor and integrity.

Fourth, the relentless call to mission. I see in each of these families the careful day-by-day reminder of their family identity and the behaviors that were expected of them, such as with the Rekabites. This was not casual engagement but a call to daily spiritual battle.

Fifth, within each of these families you see a built-in code of conduct. They lived with a certain knowledge that they were different. You see this most prominently in the Rekabites. No houses, fields, or vineyards. Living in tents.

Staying sober. Similarly, Phinehas was born in the priestly line as the grandson of Aaron. His descendants knew they were called to minister in the tabernacle and represent God's holiness to Israel.

And finally, within each of these stories, you see a different walk of life representing legacy. Perez represents the story of the guy with a tough beginning. But through the grace of God, he's able to course-correct.

In Ezra, you see the priestly line. Think of him as the ministry guy. Yet he's clearly aware of the larger family story. He's just a piece of the puzzle.

In Boaz, you see the first business guy. He's come from a long line of generational success. Yet he does not use that apparent wealth for himself. Instead, he demonstrates the kindness and compassion that we'd expect from the kinsman-redeemer.

From every walk of life, there's the opportunity for the Legacy Life. Indeed, the opportunity for generational success.

But the legacy adventures don't end with the pages of Scripture. We look at history and see that they are continuing even today. And we can learn much from their stories.

10

LEGACY FAMILIES *in* HISTORY

> Family is not just about giving life; it is about the quality of life they live in future generations.
>
> Tieman H. Dippel Jr.

His story was tragic. Shocking, even.

He approached me at one of our events and wanted to talk privately. Quietly, out of earshot of others.

He struck me as a solid, tough-minded guy. But his story spoke of his sadness. His grandfather was one of those pioneering guys, a farmer. The grandfather found a better use for the farm ground, however. He realized he had a knack for real estate development. As he invested, he went through the school of hard knocks, and his steady mistakes slowly turned to hard-earned wisdom.

Lo and behold, over time, rock by rock, shovel by shovel, the real estate business moved from surviving to sustaining to thriving. He never really considered himself successful. As many people discover, success is a summit that's never quite achieved; it's elusive and more surprising when you find yourself in a place of prosperity.

The grandfather never really acted like a guy who had arrived. A pickup truck was adequate. No need for a bigger house. No need for big vacations. No need for stock portfolios. He liked investing in dirt. You could touch it and feel it, unlike some paper portfolio.

But the ascent took a long time, and he raised his children in that same struggle. Still, he was confronted with what to do with the assets. His three children hadn't really been involved in the growth of the business, but he hoped that his son could manage things going forward on behalf of his two daughters. He had so much to teach his son.

Then the grandfather died.

The son moved in, as they say, large and in charge. He enjoyed the authority and the perks that came with it. New vehicles. It took cash to run the business, and he seemed to prosper himself. On the other hand, there never seemed to be enough for distributions to his siblings. The siblings didn't understand how that could be the case when their brother lived so well.

One of the siblings engaged a son to look into things. That son was the man standing before me, and he told the sad tale of how it took a lawsuit to get things resolved. Sibling versus sibling. Family versus family. While lawsuits may get resolved, they don't resolve the rift in families.

His situation is reflective of an American proverb that goes like this: Shirtsleeves to shirtsleeves in three generations.

It means that one generation struggles to earn wealth, the next generation spends it, and the third is back to working again. While the pattern is not always exactly three generations, the truth of the proverb is reinforced by the fact that it is repeated in virtually every culture around the world:

There's nobbut three generations atween a clog and clog. (UK)
Wealth never survives three generations. (China)
From stalls to stars to stalls. (Italy)
The third generation ruins the house. (Japan)[1]

As you read these proverbs, hear the wisdom underneath. And remember that these proverbs apply to more than financial wealth. Here's the sobering fact: Few families successfully transfer their values from one generation to the next.

In fact, I make the argument that it's easier for families to succeed generationally if they do have a business. The business forces them to keep coming back to the table to have conversations. If the business isn't making money, there's no reason to keep meeting. The business gives the family a reason to be.

If you don't have a business, then you must work extremely hard at your family purpose. I don't want to keep beating the same drum (although I really do), but you've got to have a vision, a mission, and values that you work diligently to pass from one generation to the next. In the next few pages, I'll give a few examples of legacy families in history.

Some good. Some bad. We'll look to drive home the lessons from these families.

The Vanderbilt Family—the Greatest Failure

Cornelius Vanderbilt entered the transportation business when he borrowed a hundred dollars from his mother and bought a boat.[2] He commanded passenger boats off Staten Island in 1810. For that he earned the nickname "Commodore."

His business grew from just passenger boats to include steamboats.

Steamboats gave way to railroads across America.

By all accounts, Commodore Vanderbilt was a strange mix of ambition, competition, drive, and greed. By the time of his death, the Commodore was worth $100 million—the largest fortune in America at the time, and by today's standards, a multibillion-dollar estate.

At his death in 1877, Vanderbilt believed the estate would be best managed by one child—in this case, by his oldest son, William. William inherited an 87 percent stake in New York Central, the family railroad business. Lest anyone think William was the favored child, his father typically called him a "blatherskite"—to put it lightly, the Commodore had little faith in William's abilities.

Nonetheless, if by default only, William was the choice. Commodore's dying words to William were simply: "Keep the money together." Keeping the money together didn't come without strife. Two of his siblings sued William, seeking a better share of the fortune. After six months of a much-publicized trial, William finally settled, tired of the drama.

William proved better than a blatherskite. He doubled the family fortune to $200 million. But perhaps the stress of working for his father led to his early demise. He lasted only eight years after his father's death. Contrary to his father's wishes of keeping the money together, he split the majority of the family fortune between his two eldest sons, Cornelius Vanderbilt II and William Kissam Vanderbilt.

By the time of the third generation, the descendants showed a declining passion for and interest in the business. That passion for the business was replaced by personal pleasures—yachts, summer houses, European houses, grand balls, and fast cars. One of the grandsons, George, spent his fortune on the 146,000-acre Biltmore estate in Asheville, North Carolina. He eventually ran out of money and had to start selling off land to finance his activities. Another grandson, William, said sadly, "Inherited wealth is a real handicap to happiness. . . . It has left me with nothing to hope for, with nothing definite to seek or strive for."[3]

> "Inherited wealth is a real handicap to happiness. . . . It has left me with nothing to hope for, with nothing definite to seek or strive for."
> —William Vanderbilt

By the fourth generation, the Vanderbilts were noted more for their spending than their business acumen. Reggie Vanderbilt, the son of Cornelius II, was a playboy and a gambler. He fathered Gloria Vanderbilt. Gloria's upbringing was traumatic at best. Her mom and extended family desired access to her trust fund more than they cared to raise her. Her son, Anderson Cooper, of CNN fame and the sixth generation, inherited nothing from Gloria.

By 1970, the crown jewel of the family wealth, the railroad company New York Central, declared bankruptcy. The vast family fortune was gone. Despite the Commodore's dying plea, the family could not keep the money together.

The Rothschild Family—Generations of Success

Mayer Amschel Rothschild was born in 1744 in Frankfurt, Germany. He grew up in what was called the Jewish ghetto. Jews were very much looked down upon and not seen fit to work in business. The name Rothschild came from the red shield upon their house (*zum rothen Schild*). At that time, a person's location was determined not by their house number but by different symbols or colors on the front of their house.

Growing up, Mayer appeared to be destined to become a rabbi. However, his studies were cut short when his parents died, and he instead apprenticed with a banking house. His early business career was marked by trading in coins. A key turning point came when he earned the business of Prince Wilhelm of Hesse, part of the reigning royalty. He began to serve other royal houses accordingly. By the age of forty-seven, Mayer was quite prosperous.

But his prosperity was not just for himself. Mayer believed that he should give a tenth of everything, with particular emphasis on helping the poor in the community. He helped establish a school for poor Jewish children.[4] Mayer was particularly active in supporting Jewish civil liberties. In those days, Jews faced travel restrictions and could not enjoy the benefits of citizenship. Mayer fought for their freedom and, just a year before his death, was able to achieve citizenship rights for all Jews in Germany.[5]

In addition to his philanthropy, Mayer sought opportunities for his family. He sent his five sons throughout Europe to establish other banking enterprises. His oldest son Amschel remained in Frankfurt, while his second son Salomon went to Vienna. His third son Nathan moved to London, while Carl and Jacob, the fourth and fifth sons, moved to Naples and Paris respectively. Out of the five, Nathan became the most prominent. Jacob was not far behind.

In 1810, Mayer formalized the partnership with his sons, calling the entity M. A. Rothschild and Sons. Their family crest became a fist clutching five arrows, symbolizing the concepts of Psalm 127 that children are like arrows in the hands of a warrior. They had three primary values: unity, integrity, and industry. In fact, Mayer's persistent pleas and dying instructions to his sons were, above all, to maintain family unity. Mayer himself recognized that "Jewish fortunes as a rule don't keep longer than two generations."[6]

> **Mayer's persistent pleas and dying instructions to his son were, above all, to maintain family unity.**

Over time, the Rothschild family became known for international banking, relationships with top governmental leaders, funding war efforts, trading in goods (sometimes smuggling, as the times called for it), and international payments. Their efforts were clothed in secrecy. The work of Niall Ferguson in *The House of Rothschild: Money's Prophets, 1798–1848* has done much to debunk the myths surrounding the family.

Ferguson's work in particular points out the family's emphasis on unity. After Mayer's death in 1812, the brothers faced substantial conflict. The risks that they took financially led to great challenges in business.

In his benediction to his father, Amschel, the oldest son, repeated his father's deathbed appeal: "Amschel, keep your brothers together, and you will become the richest people in Germany." After a particularly difficult period of conflict, Salomon reminded Nathan, "Our blessed father ordered us to live in peace."[7]

After Nathan passed away in 1836, a new partnership agreement was drawn up with these principles enshrined:

> We wish to offer a proof of our reverence for the holiest memory of our father, whose virtuous conduct in all of life's relations is a noble example to us all. Through pious acceptance of the higher wishes of God through faith in God's help, through conscientious honesty and indefatigable industry, this noble and philanthropic man laid the foundation of our good fortune, and when, almost forty years ago, he took his sons into partnership with him in his business, *he told them that acting in unison would be a sure means of achieving success* in their work, and always recommended fraternal concord to them as a source of divine blessing.... May our children and descendants in the future be guided by the same aim, so that with the constant maintenance of unity, the House of Rothschild may blossom and grow into full ripeness.[8]

Even outsiders to the family noted the careful attention of the brothers to steward the business as one unit for the good of the family.[9] They noted that the rule for business decisions, particularly as it related to Nathan, came down to whether it was good for the family.[10]

However, not only did they see this principle of unity as important among them, but they also saw it as a generational command. As late as 1841, Amschel reminded his other partners—many who had never met his father:

> I therefore request most urgently that you, beloved brothers and nephews, will always take care to implant in your heirs the same consciousness of concord and togetherness so that the same [spirit of] unity and co-operation continues to exist for as long is at all possible. To do so will be of benefit both to you and to your descendants. It will prevent our business interests from being split up. . . . So I ask you, for the sake of ensuring unity . . . not to make any immediate decision, but to let a few days pass first to allow tempers to cool.[11]

These foundational principles allowed the family to succeed into the next generation. They continued to fight for family unity, even to the point of encouraging marriage among cousins. They wanted to keep family capital united and safe from "outsiders."[12] The family proceeded on into a third generation, and admittedly the third generation was given to acquiring land and houses.[13] However, they remained focused on growing, and the pursuit of these assets was in part to advance their business interests in the form of entertaining clients.[14]

As the generations pressed forward, it would be foolish to say they proceeded perfectly. Their dominance in the banking world changed as other players entered the scene, and the family had some of the normal splits and disputes that plague most families. But the core remains. Their exact wealth is hard to determine because many of their holdings remain closely held, but they span a number of industries, from finance to real estate, mining, energy, wineries, and charitable work.[15]

The Kongō Gumi Story

While the Vanderbilt story is based in America, and the Rothschild story finds its roots in Germany, generations of family success or failure are not limited to those two countries. If you take a look at a list of generational family businesses around the world, you'll see they come from many countries, including France, Italy, Germany, Spain, Switzerland, Mexico, and Chile—but the oldest is Kongō Gumi in Japan.[16]

As Buddhism spread in Japan, so did the need for Buddhist temples.[17] In AD 578, the Kongō Gumi company was founded to address that need. Little did they know that their construction company would last under private family ownership for 1,400 years. In 2006, it became a subsidiary of another company. Even today, on the first and fifteenth of the month, Kongō Gumi carpenters still gather to remember and offer a prayer to their humble beginnings.

What allowed them to survive for over 1,400 years and forty generations? As a company, they were so committed to quality that a new worker could expect a ten-year apprenticeship. Becoming a master carpenter took twenty years! The carpenters organized into groups and often competed among themselves to provide the highest-quality work.

As times changed, the family and the business adapted. They moved into commercial and residential projects; they adopted different construction methods and became one of the first to adopt computer-aided design methodology.

In terms of leadership, the focus was always on maintaining family leadership. However, this did not always mean the oldest son was selected. Instead, the company focused on ability, competence, and health. They also had to get creative. One time when no suitable male leader was present, they adopted a son-in-law, and another time, they had the widow of a male leader step into the role.

By the time of the thirty-second leader, the company developed a creed that listed sixteen principles for success. These principles were a mix of business and family principles and included basic ideas such as these:

Listen to what the customer says.
Treat the customers with respect.
Do not put yourself forward.
Never fight with others.
Communicate with respect.

And at the heart of the creed: Keep and maintain the family.

Legacy Family Principles

What can we learn from these three families? The Vanderbilts—one of the greatest family legacy failures. The Rothschilds—ongoing, not perfect, family success. Kongō Gumi—forty generations of success. With each story, you see some of the principles for family success:

1. *The danger of money.* Commodore Vanderbilt's dying words were to keep the money together. But

the money was not enough to allow the family to thrive.

2. *The call to family unity.* In stark contrast to the dying wishes of Commodore Vanderbilt were the dying words of Mayer Rothschild: Stay unified. His words remind us of the priestly prayer of Jesus in John 17 where He calls for the unity of believers—that they may be one.

3. *The call to a creed.* The Kongō Gumi family had a creed that defined them for generations. The Rothschild family did the same: unity, integrity, and industry. Within that creed was the belief that we don't just serve ourselves. We place our faith and hope in God.

4. *The call to intentionally teach the next generations.* Kongō Gumi's careful apprenticeships for ten years and twenty years imply mastery of not only skill but also of values. Likewise, Nathan Rothschild wrote of passing on values: "May our children and descendants in the future be guided by the same aim so that with the constant maintenance of unity the House of Rothschild may blossom and grow into full ripeness."[18]

5. *The value of generosity.* We see little generosity consistently expressed in the Vanderbilt family; instead, they seemed to be in pursuit of the elusive "more." But the Rothschilds lived with the model of their father and the idea of responsibility to help the world around them.

6. *The power of gratitude.* We see gratitude reflected in the Rothschilds where they recognized that they were invited into a partnership with their father: "This

noble and philanthropic man laid the foundation of our good fortune, and when, almost forty years ago, he took his sons into partnership with him in his business."[19] Even today, the Kongō Gumi carpenters gather twice a month in gratitude.

7. *The recognition of our role as stewards.* Gratitude leads to recognizing that we received everything we have. We are not owners. We are stewards. All that we have, all that we are, we serve and hold in trust for the generations to come.

Please don't miss these points. None of these principles relies on money. These principles are not focused on business. Successful family legacies can be built on a clear vision, mission, and values. Witness the legacy of Abraham, Perez, the Rekabites, and Ezra.

One quick aside.

I've cited just a few families here in this chapter. I could have included hundreds of other stories. Many of them are troubling, showing the same generational failure that I've mentioned to you throughout. The Fords. The Astors. The Carnegies. If you go international, it's not hard to come up with a list: the Baring family from the UK; the Cadbury family (think chocolate) also from the UK; the Krupp family (think steel and weapons) from Germany; the Onassis family (think shipping) from Greece.[20]

One thing you'll note from these writings so far is the absence of any one strong Christian family whose faith shaped their generational view of business. One such example is a Christian Reformed Dutch community in rural Iowa. In the late 1800s, English and Scotch-Irish immigrants who had settled into Peoria, Iowa, saw their town floundering. The newly built railroad had bypassed their small settlement, leaving the settlers with little hope for growth. The town's struggles left farmers willing to sell their farmland cheap, and nearby Dutch immigrants gladly purchased the property.

However, the Dutch viewed farming differently. They "tended to take the long view, one measured in generations, not crop cycles."[21] Like any farmer, they needed to earn a profit in order to survive, but they focused more on their farm as a heritage for generations, not on the hope for a bumper crop year over year. The farmers thrived, and they soon surpassed their non-Dutch neighbors. They used their new prosperity to build up the community, forming a Christian Reformed Church and a private school to pass on their faith and heritage to future generations.

Let me suggest that we need more stories of faithful families who have a generational vision. People who see themselves as living out a godly purpose and impacting the world around them for generations. My family is just now into our fifth generation. At a personal level, I know of one other Christian family business that is into its sixth generation.

We've seen many families start out as Christian but end up in a far different place. That's why we've written this book. To learn from their mistakes.

But what if you feel you've already messed up your legacy? What if, as you read, you see yourself and your family reflected more in the stories of failure than of success? In the next chapter, we will examine what to do when it seems that our legacy is too far gone. If all seems lost, rest assured—all is never lost. But the way up will require us to first descend.

11

A LEGACY *from* BROKENNESS

> But there was no need to be ashamed of tears, for tears bore witness that a man had the greatest of courage, the courage to suffer.
>
> Viktor Frankl, *Man's Search for Meaning*

This might be the hardest chapter to write.

Some might look at me and think, "Well, David, it's great for you to write about legacy. I mean, look at you! You've got a great family. Everyone is a believer. You've got kids, grandkids, and great-grandkids. You've had a great marriage. To top it off, pretty much every member lives near you!" And it's true; out of our nearly fifty family members in all four generations, all live in Oklahoma City.

I'll admit it. I'm blessed.

But life's not perfect. I nearly went bankrupt in 1986. At the start of the COVID-19 pandemic, for a time I had great fears over the mounting bills while our stores were shut down. Barbara and I have been married for sixty-three years, and if you think we didn't have some tough times—well, you'd be quite mistaken. And on top of all that, we've got three kids, three in-laws, ten grandchildren (most of them married), and as for great-grandchildren, at last count . . . well, I'd better not go there because the number is changing all the time. I'll just say I've got great-grandchildren numbering in the high teens. All of this means that we are a family. Like any family, we have struggles, disappointments, questions of faith, and disagreements.

These are the realities of being a family.

My granddaughter Lauren and her husband Michael wrote a book about how their perfect little world wasn't so perfect after all. They got married with all the hope and vigor of youth. Michael sometimes likes to joke that he had his life all figured out at age seven. He met Lauren at school then. At show-and-tell, he came dressed in a suit with his Bible. He jokes that he knew who he was going to marry, and he knew his vocation—a Bible preacher!

Along the way, life happened.

When Michael was in college, his dad (and Michael's hero) divorced his mom. That shattered his world and was his first crisis of faith. Was this thing called the Bible and what it stood for—hope, faith, love, and family—all real?

While the crisis drove him deeper into his faith, the journey was just beginning.

He and Lauren did in fact get married. Michael got his pastoral job. Lauren was happy working with Hobby Lobby.

After about four years of marriage, they looked into international adoption. After five years of pursuing things internationally, nothing had happened.

So, they changed plans and figured they'd try to get pregnant instead. After months of no success, they began looking to doctors to determine whether their dreams needed a jump start. The medical testing was not positive for their future hope of having biological children.

Their perfect plan of education, marriage, house, career, children sat in a frustrated holding pattern.

Beyond their control.

They went back to the adoption route, and finally, it was a happy scene when they got the news that they could adopt their daughter Zion from China. That happiness continued. Until life interrupted.

Just one month into bringing Zion home, she was undergoing a standard medical screening when they discovered a tumor on Zion's liver. She had cancer. Michael and Lauren went from happy, jubilant adoptive parents to parents in the cancer ward, talking to doctors, oncologists, and nurses and combing the internet for solutions.

Let's face it. As Christians, we're supposed to have faith, but when it comes to our kids, we worry. They faced surgery and chemotherapy. Finally, their daughter was better, but anytime you go through something like that, it lingers in the back of your mind. But back to a happy story, right?

They wanted to continue growing their family, so they pursued a second adoption, this time domestic. Within a few weeks of completing their paperwork, they got a call that a mother had chosen them to parent her baby boy.

They named him Ezra. For twelve months, they changed the diapers, nursed him, sang him to sleep, got up early with him, loved him. Zion became a big sister. But before the adoption could be finalized, the court intervened. They ruled that Ezra would be handed over to a biological family member who decided he wanted to parent after all.

In a matter of hours, Ezra was gone. Zion never got to say goodbye to Ezra.

It is not what they wanted. It is not what they planned. It is not the story they would have written.

Their story is part of our family story, and Michael and Lauren published their story in a book called *Beyond Our Control: Let Go of Unmet Expectations, Overcome Anxiety, and Discover Intimacy with God*.[1]

Every family has their story. I know this. And in that story are moments of brokenness. It's the nature of this life we live.

Our Broken Legacies

In the events that Bill and I host for leaders across the country, people come up to us after the sessions and tell us the most incredible stories. Not all of them are good stories, and their stories sometimes leave us with more questions than answers.

The lost children. It's the most common heartbreak that we hear. Children who walk away from the faith. Sometimes that walking away is just a life apart from faith and church. Sometimes that walking away looks like addictions and other heartrending behaviors. But every departure leads to the same question: "We did our best, so how did we get here?" I had one father remark bitterly, "Legacy?! All of my children are going to hell. What do I do?"

The success trap. Some tell us of regrets from pursuing worldly success. Their great sadness is that they climbed the ladder of success, only to find it was leaning against the proverbial wrong building. Some have said the greatest failure is to succeed at the things that don't matter. Pursuing the things of the world can choke the word of God and produce emptiness. Bill tells me of a call he got from a young man who was succeeding wildly at his business—they had 100 percent growth and all the outward trappings to go with it. He bought a massive house. However, by the time he acquired it, he had nothing to put in it. Barely a few sticks of furniture. His wife didn't want the life he was building. He was alone.

The lost years. Sometimes people come up to tell us about their early faith in Christ, followed by years of wandering. Or the years when they never knew Christ at all. One woman told us of the years of praying for her lost husband. While the sweetness of a faith regained or a newfound faith are wonderful, they make us pause and wonder about those lost years and what might have been.

The personal failures. This is one of the hard ones. What happens when the person you thought you were proves to be different from your own actions? Sometimes these are failures of personal integrity. Sometimes these are failures of commitment. I had one lawyer tell me simply that he'd probably still be married to his first wife if he had chosen to work less. Still another told me of the loss of his marriage because of his lack of sole commitment to his wife.

The generosity challenge. I remember one young man who came into one of our meetings, and he was proud. He was giving 11 percent of his income, and he thought that was great. But his wife and his kids weren't involved. It was just him, and about him. He was keeping 89 percent of his income for himself. He'd never thought that 100 percent of his income belonged to God and that he could consider giving more. He thought about the money he now considered wasted on himself and his stuff. He went home from the meeting intent on making a change.

The ownership challenge. For years, I always said that God was the owner of everything—including my business. While that's what I said, my actions were no different from the rest of the world. I still treated the business as my own. I'd gone down the road of giving my children stock in the business without knowing how it might impact them and the generations to come. Thankfully, when we realized our error, they were willing to work with us to create a new trust that superseded and absorbed the old trusts.

We've had so many people come up and tell us they wish they had learned the concept of ownership versus stewardship sooner. They regret giving too much to their children. One family told me about their decision to give ownership interests in their business to their children and grandchildren. Those interests had grown and blossomed, and the dividends from those interests had allowed their children to stop working. Many of their grandchildren were no longer working. That lost drive and creativity had moved many of them to a place not of contentment but of wanting more. Gifts to children who are not prepared to handle wealth can be a great curse.

Broken (and Redeemed) Legacies in the Bible

Instead of being honest and defending their wives, Abraham and Isaac both let other men take their wives.

Jacob cheated his brother to gain the inheritance.

Jacob's kids sold their brother into slavery.

Moses lived in the palace of the pharaoh. Then he murdered a man. He fled to the wilderness where he tended sheep. For forty years.

Moses, the humblest man on the face of the earth, rose up in anger and struck the rock instead of speaking to it. He showed his authority before men, but it cost him the promised land.

When the spies entered the promised land, Rahab, a prostitute, had to rescue them.

Joshua, mentored by Moses, is known as the great conqueror. But on his watch, one of his men confiscated forbidden goods, which led to a great defeat and a loss of confidence in his leadership. Then he allowed Israel to negotiate a peace treaty with a neighboring tribe—all without consulting God. Oops.

Eli was the leading priest of his day, but he had two sons who were scoundrels and slept with prostitutes.

Likewise, when the prophet Samuel appointed his two sons as Israel's leaders, they turned out to be dishonest cheats, accepting bribes and perverting justice.

David was the long-sought-after king. Yet his own family was messed up. One of his sons raped his half sister. Another son murdered the brother that committed rape. It gets worse. David's own son attempted to kill him and take the kingdom from him. David also committed adultery, then he tried to cover it up. When that failed, he committed murder.

Hosea was asked to marry a prostitute.

Jeremiah was asked to remain single, to not have a family, to not go to weddings, feasts, or funerals.

Daniel spent his life in exile.

Jesus the Messiah was born to a carpenter and a teenage girl who were outcasts in their own village.

Peter, dubbed "the Rock," denied Jesus not once, but three times.

The disciples abandoned Jesus in His hour of need.

Paul murdered Christians.

What great legacy stories, right? Talk about broken legacies. But here's the crazy thing. Somehow, God can take every broken legacy and redeem it. It may not be right away. It may take time. It may take generations.

Think about Moses. He must've had nightmares about the man he murdered. He probably relived a thousand times the flash of burning anger and the rash action of raising his hand against a man mistreating a fellow Israelite. When the deed was complete, Moses did his best to cover his tracks. But although the sand could cover the dead body, it could not cover the fear in his heart—the fear of being found out. Even worse, when his name appeared on the wanted posters, Moses fled in terror. He left everything behind.

> **Somehow, God can take every broken legacy and redeem it.**

And for forty years, Moses lived in the desert wilderness. While God gave him some relief through a new father-in-law, a wife, and children, I imagine the nights were the worst. I wonder if the murder played in his head every night, like a nightmare he couldn't rid himself of. Or if, during the still moments of shepherding, he stared off into the distance and wondered how God could ever use a man like him.

Was it any wonder that when it was finally time to go to Egypt, Moses's confidence waned? He asked God, "Why is anyone ever going to believe me?" He tried to get out of the assignment by claiming that he was afraid of public speaking. But God took a broken-down, confidence-stricken Moses and started to rebuild him and restore him. Time after time in front of Pharaoh, Moses saw God work miracle after miracle.

Pharaoh's heart did not turn; it remained hard, unchanged, and unable to bear any fruit. But Moses? Well, it was *his* heart that was changing. Even after God delivered the Israelites from Egypt, Moses continued to see waters part, rocks quench thirst, and manna fall from heaven. He began to believe. It wasn't too long before he no longer needed Aaron as a crutch. Moses could speak on his own. From the scared shepherd in Exodus 3 to the leader at the end of Exodus 34, God transformed a broken legacy into a redeemed legacy. Moses then, by the grace of God, delivered a powerful charge to his people.

What about David? Like Moses, he was called to greatness, to become the faithful king that Israel needed. David's family failures would leave most of us undone. But his adultery with Bathsheba was perhaps the movie reel that most played over and over in his mind. A moment of lust led to an improper relationship. The crime and its cover-up were so repulsive that the Lord sent Nathan the prophet to bring him everyone's worst nightmare: *What you think you have done in private, I'll reveal to the world.*

How do you redeem that messed-up story? I think Psalm 51 is part of that redemption. We hear David's anguish: "Have mercy on me, O God, according to your unfailing love" (v. 1). His prayer of confession is not the ritual listing of misdeeds. No, David *feels* his sin. He's covered with it like the black soot of a polluted chimney. He pleads, "Wash away all my iniquity and cleanse me from all my sin" (v. 2). His is the glad heart of the broken restored to relationship—"restore to me the joy of your salvation" (v. 12)—and one with resolve for a better future—"Create in me a pure heart, O God, and renew a steadfast spirit within me" (v. 10).

Psalm 51 stands as a reminder to every soul who has failed before God. It's the pathway for how the utter blackness of our sin can be washed away and a right relationship can be restored before God.

> When the trials of this life seem to crush us, in the bigger picture, in the Lord's grand narrative, He can always—always—redeem and restore.

And that's really the sum of the broken legacy. God has the ability to restore. Yes, Rahab's a prostitute, but she marries into the line of Christ and brings children to that line. Despite some early failures, Joshua completes the assignment given to him and brings Israel into the promised land. Samuel's failures with his own sons remind us how desperately we need the one true and faithful High Priest. Hosea's unfaithful marriage is a sign pointing to a right relationship with the pure bride. Jeremiah's singleness helped shape a generation. Daniel's exile reminds us of a people longing for home. Joseph and Mary? Although they were temporary outcasts in their earthly village, they'll be revered in heaven for their faith. Peter denied Christ, but his resolve to lead launched the church age. Paul's murderous past allowed him to stand before kings with credibility and complete his calling.

Here's what I'm trying to say. In the moment, it may seem that all is lost. Whether through our own brutal failures or as the circumstances of life seem to pummel us in the day-to-day, the whisper in each of these stories is a simple message: When the trials of this life seem to crush us, in the bigger picture, in the Lord's grand narrative, He can always—always—redeem and restore.

That's the power of the broken legacy.

It's Not Too Late to Start

I know there are some who will arrive at this place in the chapter and ask, "But how? All is lost. It seems too late." Here's my straightforward advice: Start where you are. Then entrust the results to God.

Starting may look like repairing the past. Praying a prayer of repentance like David. A plea to "wash me and make me clean." Making a phone call to repair and renew a relationship. It may start with daily prayer for others. It may just mean a commitment to be in God's Word every day. It could mean obeying the nudge that God has been giving you all these years. Maybe it's finally resolving that ownership question and freeing yourself to be God's steward. Maybe still it's being generous with what you have.

Or perhaps you feel that all is lost. Someone has seemingly died too young. You are facing grief you never imagined. There is no hope of salvaging a legacy.

Perhaps you've heard of the story of Horatio Spafford.[2] He was a lawyer and businessman in Chicago, where he had extensive real estate holdings. He was known as a kind and generous man who supported various missions, including the YMCA and the Presbyterian Theological Seminary. Despite his successes, in October 1871, Spafford's real estate holdings, including his law office, were essentially wiped out by the infamous Great Chicago Fire.

Even though he was mired in debt, by November 1873, Spafford felt it necessary to get his wife, Anna, and four daughters (Annie, eleven; Margaret, nine; Elizabeth, five; and Tanetta, two) away from their dreary circumstances. They were to set sail for Europe aboard the *Ville du Havre*, a large ship well acquainted with the long Atlantic voyage. At the last minute, Horatio was delayed when an opportunity arose to sell some of his fire-stricken properties.

The voyage began on November 15, 1873. Inexplicably, at 2 a.m. on November 22, 1873, the *Ville du Havre* was struck squarely by the *Loch Earn*. The collision sprang a twelve-foot hole in the *Ville*, and water came pouring in, while despairing passengers clad only in nightgowns rushed to the deck. The ship sank within twelve minutes.

Only Anna survived. When she reached port, she sent a telegram to Horatio, telling him of their great loss: "Saved alone. What shall I do?" In dealing with their grief, both Anna and Horatio took to writing. It was Horatio, when reflecting upon the loss of his four daughters, who penned the now famous words:

> When peace, like a river, attendeth my way,
> When sorrows like sea billows roll

> Whatever my lot, Thou hast taught me to say,
> It is well, it is well with my soul.

Spafford's hymn, now his legacy, has been sung in countless church services around the globe. Its words provide hope to those in trial and suffering. It's been a beacon of hope for many a mourner in funeral services far and wide. His loss became his legacy.

Spafford's story reminds us that in God's bigger picture, He is always using the bigger story to impact the world for His greater glory.

So don't give up. Stay the course. Keep your eyes fixed on home.

12

HEAVEN *in* SIGHT

> All we have to decide is what to do with the time given to us.
>
> J. R. R. Tolkien, *The Fellowship of the Ring*

Have you ever gone on a long journey?
Not long before the writing of this book was complete, Barbara and I were able to go on an overseas cruise. We planned the trip far in advance. Usually, you've got to be nine months out to get the selection and pricing you want. We looked at all the options—where to go, what to do, how much it would cost, who we'd go with. Once we'd done our research, we made the big plunge, put down our deposit, and promptly forgot about it.

We went back to work, which is always busy. There were events, speaking engagements, and of course family activities. There was church and the activities that go with that, and we'd still take the occasional weekend trip. Every now and then, our long journey popped up in the back of our minds. But it was too far and too distant to do anything about it.

But the months did pass. Time and distance always have a way of catching up. With thirty days to go, we got our passports out, checked the flight schedules again, looked at our connections, and began to track weather forecasts. Soon we were just a week out, then a few days out, and some of that familiar trip anxiety set in.

We started to get serious—getting out suitcases, finding adapters, laying out clothes for all kinds of weather conditions, and of course packing the little pills and potions that everyone has. We double-checked those flights, flight connections, and airport parking.

The trip was on our minds now. We'd even read the trip brochure. We didn't want to miss packing anything we might really need.

Finally, it was time. Our checklists were complete, suitcases full, boarding passes printed (yes, we still print them), parking complete, and security passed. We were off to the first flight. All good. But things can never go perfectly when traveling, right? Sure enough, our second flight was late—for unknown reasons, whether maintenance, weather, pilots, or attendants. It didn't matter. We missed our connection in London.

Things wouldn't have been so bad, but we had a ship to catch—a deadline. Worse, our travel agent was about seven hours behind us. After what seemed like countless calls, we finally got a flight, but it meant that we would spend seven more hours in the airport. Waiting. Jet-lagged. It's hard to sleep in airport chairs. We boarded our next flight bleary-eyed but grateful, finally arriving at our destination about ten hours late.

The next morning, still weary, we boarded our ship, and the adventure began. Like so many things in life, the fun part seemed to speed by. We moved from country to country, port to port, almost effortlessly. Our days passed quickly with tours and excursions, and our heads were filled with all the histories of the countries we visited. Much of it was information we likely would never use again. Still, we loved the old buildings—it felt like touching history.

Most of the time we loved the new cuisines, although I'd be lying if I didn't say that it was pretty wonderful when we could grab a cheeseburger and fries. In the evenings, we got to enjoy some great shows, even a great comedian.

When you're having fun like that, the days pass quickly, and going home sneaks up on you. We started the same routine again, repacking our suitcases and double-checking flights, checkout procedures, and transportation to the airport. The flights home came without any drama . . . they were just long. It always seems to take such a long time to get home. When the last flight landed, we collected our luggage and, just a little numb, made our way to our car, suitcases in tow.

While it's a short drive home, and we've made it a thousand times, it always seems the longest when you've been away for so long. Get the right exit, make the right turn, down the long drive, pop the trunk, unload the suitcases, and burst through the front door. We drop everything, flipping on lights, and we head to our familiar living room, our familiar couch. We sink in, lean back, and let out the longest sigh.

Finally home.

We've Lost Sight of Home

As I write, I wonder if you are like me. We book our trip but forget about it. We accept the joy of salvation but forget about the journey, let alone the destination. Is it enough to punch our ticket but live with so little of heaven in sight?

As Nathan Knight writes in his article "How Often Do You Think About Heaven?":

> Matthew Westerholm studied the difference between songs used in American churches from 2000–2015 and those used from 1737–1960. His conclusion? "Among many similarities, one difference was striking: the topic of heaven, which once was frequently and richly sung about, has now all but disappeared."[1]

Knight puts a different spin on it by pointing out that in the Bible, the hope of heaven is referenced 387 times out of 7,957 verses. By comparison, the concept of hell is only referenced 150–160 times and marriage just 30–40 times.

> **We accept the joy of salvation but forget about the journey, let alone the destination.**

Heaven is a big deal.

Here's an interesting fact. Do a search of the word *heaven* in the Bible. What do you come up with? Throughout the early part of the Scriptures—the first five books of the Bible—heaven is referred to 54 times.[2] That shouldn't surprise us given that the world was starting up and the concept of heaven was literally staring them in the face.

But when you turn to Joshua, when Israel is busy conquering the promised land, heaven is mentioned just once. During the period of the judges, when Israel is up and down in their relationship with God, heaven is mentioned just 3 times. That similar scarcity continues through the early period of the kings, and it is not until David ascends the throne that we see a marked difference. The vast majority of the psalms are written by David or people that he influenced, like Asaph or the sons of Korah.[3] The Psalms explode with 76 verses on heaven!

Is it any wonder that David is considered a man after God's own heart?

There is only one other book with a similar explosion. It's the book of Matthew, with another 76 references. That shouldn't surprise us. In fact, right from the opening, John the Baptist tells his audiences to "repent, for the kingdom of heaven has come near" (Matt. 3:2). Jesus repeated that same thought a chapter later: "Repent, for the kingdom of heaven has come near" (Matt. 4:17). In fact, if you include all the references to heaven throughout the Gospels and the book of Acts, it comes to a whopping 151 references.

When we consider the person who lived the ultimate Legacy Life, it should not surprise us that Jesus was pointing His disciples to look to heaven. The Beatitudes, for instance, give us some of that kingdom code that Jesus sought to instill in His disciples:

Be humble—poor in spirit (Matt. 5:3).
It's okay to be persecuted for living a life of faith (Matt. 5:10, 12).
In a dim world, shine bright and show God to others (Matt. 5:16).

Teach others about the kingdom of heaven (Matt. 5:19).

Live by a higher standard—righteousness—than even the religious leaders (Matt. 5:20).

Give to the needy, pray, and fast with the right motivation—to bring God glory, not yourself (Matt. 6:1–8).

Invest in eternal things, not the things of this world that rust away (Matt. 6:19–21).

It seems to me that Jesus was doing all that He could to shake up His disciples.

He was trying to get His disciples to take their eyes off this world and the way things are done here and look toward heaven.

But Jesus was not the only one. I suppose if there's anyone else who might be looked to for a Legacy Life example, it would have to be the apostle Paul. What was his urging? Paul told the Philippian believers, "But our citizenship is in heaven" (Phil. 3:20). He repeated the same message to the church in Ephesus, telling them that they were "fellow citizens with God's people and also members of his household" (Eph. 2:19).

Much of Philippians 3 might be considered Paul's legacy creed. Let me issue a disclaimer first. I'm going to quote a long passage. To be fair, it would be easy to skip over, and you might say to yourself, "I've read these words before." But read them now—slowly—maybe even a few times. Read them with a legacy lens. Paul reminds us that we should leave the stuff of this world behind—all the praise, all the acclaim—and look forward, press on toward the goal:

> But whatever was gain to me I count as loss for the sake of Christ. More than that, I count all things as loss compared to

the surpassing excellence of knowing Christ Jesus my Lord, for whom I have lost all things. I consider them rubbish, that I may gain Christ and be found in Him, not having my own righteousness from the law, but that which is through faith in Christ, the righteousness from God on the basis of faith.

I want to know Christ and the power of His resurrection and the fellowship of His sufferings, being conformed to Him in His death, and so, somehow, to attain to the resurrection from the dead.

Not that I have already obtained all this, or have already been made perfect, but I press on to take hold of that for which Christ Jesus took hold of me. Brothers, I do not consider myself yet to have taken hold of it. But one thing I do: Forgetting what is behind and straining toward what is ahead, I press on toward the goal to win the prize of God's heavenly calling in Christ Jesus. (Phil. 3:7–13 BSB)

When you consider that Paul wrote this while in prison and likely facing his own death, his legacy message strikes home.[4] But Paul's message of looking forward in Philippians 3 does not stand alone. He repeats the message more graphically in 2 Corinthians 5:10, where he says, "For we must all appear before the judgment seat of Christ, so that each of us may receive what is due us for the things done while in the body, whether good or bad." In his earlier letter to them in 1 Corinthians, Paul describes standing before the judgment seat as a time when the deeds we have done in the body will be judged. Even though our salvation is secure, our deeds will be tested: "And the fire will test the quality of each person's work. If what has been built survives, the builder will receive a reward. If it is burned up, the builder will suffer loss but yet will be saved—even though only as one escaping through the flames" (3:13–15).

This recognition that all that we've set in motion will be tested by fire is sobering. And motivating. I want to build for what lasts. I want to build for the Legacy Life.

How do we recover, then, this vision of the power of heaven? The power of home?

Recovering the Power of Heaven

Home is the familiar ache we all live with. No matter how good our journey, Jesus understood that we would always long to be home with Him. Perhaps no one understood this longing for home better than John. He's described as the disciple whom Jesus loved (John 13:23). It's not surprising to me that almost half of John's Gospel is focused on the end of Jesus's life.

Why so much focus on the end?

It's at the end of your life that you offer your legacy words. They are your parting words. Your last instructions. Just in case you missed anything. And John is careful to write it all down. I think that of all the Gospels, John's best captures the heart and emotion of Jesus. You can almost touch the intimacy of the moment, as the Rabbi, the Master, the Teacher feels the pain of His students and seeks to comfort them.

In John 14, we get a glimpse into that upper room. Jesus sees and feels the anguish of His friends and calls to them: "Do not let your hearts be troubled" (v. 1). And why shouldn't they be troubled? Because "My Father's house has many rooms; if that were not so, would I have told you that I am going there to prepare a place for you?" (v. 2). He's giving them the hope of heaven. He's telling them, "There's room for you there, and I'm going to get it ready."

Despite Jesus's assurance, Thomas, ever the doubting one, cries out, "Lord, we don't know where you are going, so how can we know the way?" (v. 5). Thomas's question seems to trigger a flood of questions between students and Rabbi—all of them seeking reassurance. In the conversation that takes place, here's a sampling of the comfort Jesus offers:

I'm going away.
Your grief is going to turn to joy.
There's a place for you in my Father's house.
I will come back and take you to be with me.
I will not leave you as orphans. I will come to you.
I'll send the Holy Spirit.
I call you friends.
I chose you. I appointed you.
I have chosen you out of the world.

Even after all these instructions, the disciples still don't get it. By Acts 1, they are still asking if Jesus is going to bring military victory. As Jesus ascends to heaven, they stand dumbfounded, lost, not knowing what to do. It takes two angels to set the script right: "Why do you stand here looking into the sky? This same Jesus, who has been taken from you into heaven, will come back in the same way you have seen him go into heaven" (Acts 1:11).

The angels point them toward home.

To be honest, I get a little giddy at this point when I look at what happened next. The power of the Holy Spirit came upon them. They preached the story of Christ—His birth, His death, His burial, and His resurrection. And people responded. The church was birthed, and the gospel message spread.

The spread did not occur without cost or suffering. Sometimes it meant jail and threats of death. Sometimes it cost them their lives. Stephen was the first to die—at the hands of Paul, no less. Paul's own diligence in persecution would only be matched later by his diligence in carrying out his call.

Even as the persecution arrived, the church dispersed. Strategically. To all parts of the Roman world and beyond. Seeds were sown. Churches started. Churches struggled. Churches thrived, and with it all, the relentless drumbeat of a simple message—the gospel, the good news that Jesus the Christ offers restoration and redemption for all those who would confess and believe.

> **Jesus pointed His disciples to home and the vision of a place where all that is broken would be restored.**

Today, we experience the benefits of Jesus setting in motion the greatest legacy of all time: the Legacy Life. He pointed His disciples to home and the vision of a place where all that is broken would be restored.

What kept the disciples going in the midst of all these trials? Why did they not quit? Why did they not opt for a retirement home by the sea? Maybe a few rounds of golf in the late morning? No, they were fueled by a fire, a vision of home.

Paul said it this way: "We know that the whole creation has been groaning together in the pains of childbirth until now. And not only the creation, but we ourselves, who have the firstfruits of the Spirit, groan inwardly as we wait eagerly for adoption as sons, the redemption of our bodies. For in this hope we were saved" (Rom. 8:22–24 ESV).

How do we recover the hope of heaven? How do we keep moving toward home? I could offer you all the wonderful pictures of heaven offered by the book of Revelation.

No more crying. No more tears. No more pain.

Being always in the presence of God.

No darkness. Always light.

Streets of gold.

You get the picture. It's going to be a pretty wonderful place. But even as much as I might try to describe heaven, I'll fail. It's beyond our finite minds to comprehend the infinite.

So I think it best to describe heaven like this. We have to go back all the way to Eden, the time before the fall, when all was good and right, and the long journey hadn't yet started. And in the cool of the garden, God the Father is there with us, walking and talking in fellowship. It's a good and sweet conversation. Because He knows us. He cares for us, and we feel safe. We feel that we belong. Sometimes there's laughter as only good friends can enjoy.

You see, we are *finally home*.

Keep heaven in sight as you pursue the eternal life to which you were called today, my friends. And you will live the Legacy Life.

Closing Thoughts

The eternal ache.

We all have it. God put it inside of us. It's the recognition that this earth is not our home. We have a longing for something more. In this life, we intuitively look for

Meaning

Connection

Belonging

A life of significance

Work that makes a difference

We long for home—that place of belonging with our eternal Father who loves us completely, knows us completely, and has desires for us that are far bigger than our own.

The Scriptures teach us that God looks at our life and the life of our family with a generational lens.

He sees us having a generational impact. Generations of influence.

If you have children, God sees your descendants a hundred years from now, a thousand years from now. Even if you don't have children, His vision for your life is unchanged—He sees thousands of lives, thousands of generations affected by your legacy.

That's mind-boggling.

Here's the thing. God only asks you to start right where you are. And it is never too late! Be faithful with whatever He has put in front of you. There are some very practical things for you to do:

1. Change your lens to a generational worldview for your life and your family.
2. Craft a vision, mission, and values statement, as well as your code of conduct, then review it and live it out daily, weekly. Faithfulness yields big results generations from now.
3. Know and tell your stories. Repair the past.

But there is one more thing to remember. You cannot live the Legacy Life—that's right, *cannot*—other than by the grace of God. And you cannot live the Legacy Life unless your life is pointed toward heaven.

Because legacy is what you set in motion. For that day—that day in heaven.

My prayer is simply this. If you don't know Jesus, satisfy the eternal ache by confessing the fact that you've missed the mark and that you believe with all your heart that Jesus died on a cross for your sin. Ask Him to forgive you and to be part of your life.

Romans 10:9 says it simply: "If you declare with your mouth, 'Jesus is Lord,' and believe in your heart that God raised him from the dead, you will be saved."

If you do so, then you will satisfy the eternal ache. And you'll be on the path to generational blessing. You'll never regret it.

And one last thing. If we get this right—this generational vision—thousands of people who are faithful with what God puts in front of them, who practically live out their vision, mission, and values, who live by a code, well,

we
change
the world.

All because of living a Legacy Life.

APPENDIX

SAMPLE VISION, MISSION, *and* VALUES STATEMENTS

GREEN FAMILY

Vision

To go on the adventure of impacting our world for Christ.

Mission

To love God intimately. To live extravagant generosity.

Values

God

Family

Others

HIGH FAMILY

Vision

Disciples Everywhere for Generations

Mission

Rooted in Christ, Abounding in Gratitude

Values

God's Word—the truth that sets you free

Generosity—generosity brings joy

Adventure—a dangerous and uncertain undertaking

Story—connected to the divine narrative

Restoration—put back into place

Code

We will communicate.

We will deal with the hurts.

Our goal is restoration.

MAGAÑA FAMILY

Vision

Magnifying Christ, enjoying one another *por siempre.*

Mission

Pursue kindness, love joyfully, and walk humbly with the Lord.

Values

Faith—Believe the Lord even when life is a question mark.

Forgiveness—Grace upon grace. We forgive much because we've been forgiven of much.

Generosity—We give up the things we love for the things we love even more.

Hospitality—You always have a place to belong here.

Fun—We choose to see the best.

Code

We are on the same team.

We treat one another with kindness.

We listen to understand.

We forgive early.

We do the right thing.

We can still enjoy one another today.

MCELVEEN FAMILY

Vision

Touch millions together. Raise Jesus forever.

Mission

Serve souls. Praise God.

Values

Chase God.

Stand strong.

Love our crew.

Embrace others.

Acknowledgments

It is always dangerous to undertake recognizing those who make a manuscript like this possible. We'd like to thank our agent, Tom Dean, who was willing to listen to the initial idea and give encouragement to the thought of another book and the value it could bring to so many.

Tom was then willing to take that little flame of an idea to Brian Vos, the editorial director at Baker Books. Brian was a great coach, challenged our ideas, and helped shape them into a final product. Along the way, the rest of the team at Baker Books gave us feedback and thoughtful commentary. We are better because of having worked with them.

To get a book like this across the goal line is not a small undertaking. Ruthie Burrell of Rooted Biography did the editing for *The Legacy Life Devotional*, and Annika Bergen of Dream Communications did a wonderful job putting up with the writing and rewriting, editing, and moving around of ideas, paragraphs, and chapters.

We also want to acknowledge the hundreds of families who have attended our leadership events at Hobby Lobby over the years. Your willingness to leave the comfort of your homes and the busy workday life of your own speaks volumes to us. From you, we've learned of your own stories, and the wrestling toward lives of meaning.

Notes

Chapter 1 Searching for Purpose, Searching for Legacy

1. "Nazareth," Bible Places, accessed November 15, 2024, https://www.bibleplaces.com/nazareth/.

2. Magnus Olofsson, "The Swedish Army in the Napoleonic Wars," The Napoleon Series, April 2008, https://www.napoleon-series.org/military-info/organization/Sweden/Organization/c_swedisharmy.html.

3. Göran Frilund, "The Swedish Navy 1788–1809," The Final War, accessed October 7, 2024, https://www.multi.fi/~goranfri/navalwar.html.

4. Henrik Johansson, "Visingsö Oak Forest," Atlas Obscura, June 14, 2017, https://www.atlasobscura.com/places/visingso-oak-forest.

5. Johansson, "Visingsö Oak Forest."

6. Dennis Swanberg, *Planting Shade Trees: Not Everyone Can Be a Legend but Everyone Can Leave a Legacy* (Swanberg Inc., 2014), 13–14.

7. "illumiNations," Museum of the Bible, accessed October 7, 2024, www.museumofthebible.org/illuminations.

8. "William and Clara Leslie Papers," American Baptist Historical Society, accessed October 7, 2024, https://libraries.mercer.edu/archivesspace/repositories/2/resources/578.

9. Mark Ellis, "Missionary Died Thinking He Was a Failure," International Orality Network, accessed October 7, 2024, https://orality.net/content/missionary-died-thinking-he-was-a-failure/.

Chapter 2 Short-Term Thinking

1. Anthony Cardillo, "How Many Google Searches Are There Per Day? (August 2024)," Exploding Topics, accessed August 9, 2024, https://explodingtopics.com/blog/google-searches-per-day.

2. "70 Addiction to Cell Phone Statistics, Facts & Demographics," Urban Recovery, December 1, 2023, https://www.urbanrecovery.com/blog/addiction-to-cell-phone-statistics.

3. Adam Hayes, "The Human Attention Span," Wyzowl, accessed October 8, 2024, https://www.wyzowl.com/human-attention-span/.

4. Eva M. Krockow, "How Many Decisions Do We Make Each Day?," Psychology Today, September 27, 2018, https://www.psychologytoday.com/us/blog/stretching-theory/201809/how-many-decisions-do-we-make-each-day.

5. "Global Study: 70% of Business Leaders Would Prefer a Robot to Make Their Decisions," PR Newswire, April 19, 2023, https://www.prnewswire.com/news-releases/global-study-70-of-business-leaders-would-prefer-a-robot-to-make-their-decisions-301799591.html.

6. Petroc Taylor, "Amount of Data Created, Consumed, and Stored 2010–2020, with Forecasts to 2025," Statista, November 21, 2024, https://www.statista.com/statistics/871513/worldwide-data-created/.

7. Jamie Hampton, "Report: 80% of Global Workers Experience Information Overload," Big Data Wire, August 18, 2022, https://www.datanami.com/2022/08/18/report-80-of-global-workers-experience-information-overload/.

8. Andrew P. Smith and Hasah Alheneidi, "The Internet and Loneliness," *AMA Journal of Ethics* 25, no. 11 (November 2023), https://doi.org/10.1001/amajethics.2023.833.

9. "Exploring the Recent Rise of Social Anxiety Disorder," Seattle Anxiety Specialists, February 25, 2023, https://seattleanxiety.com/psychiatrist/2023/2/24/exploring-the-recent-rise-of-social-anxiety-disorder.

10. Emily Brignone, Daniel R. George, and Lawrence Sinoway, et al., "Trends in the Diagnosis of Diseases of Despair in the United States, 2009–2018: A Retrospective Cohort Study," *BMJ Open* 10, no. 10 (2020), https://doi.org/10.1136/bmjopen-2020-037679.

11. Sally C. Curtin, Matthew F. Garnett, and Farida B. Ahmad, "Provisional Numbers and Rates of Suicide by Month and Demographic Characteristics: United States, 2021," *Vital Statistics Rapid Release* 24 (September 2022), https://www.cdc.gov/nchs/data/vsrr/vsrr024.pdf.

12. Devin Clemens, "Japan's Four Oldest Family Businesses," *Tharawat Magazine*, July 10, 2019, https://www.tharawat-magazine.com/facts/japans-four-oldest-family-businesses/.

13. Irene Herrera, "Building on Tradition—1,400 Years of a Family Business," *Works That Work* 3 (2014), https://worksthatwork.com/3/kongo-gumi.

14. "Germany's 50 Oldest Family Businesses," Stiftung Familienunternehmen, December 13, 2021, https://www.familienunternehmen.de/en/news/overcoming-crises-for-centuries.

15. "Family Businesses in Italy Trek," SC Johnson College of Business, accessed October 8, 2024, https://www.johnson.cornell.edu/smith-family-business-initiative-at-cornell/students/family-businesses-in-italy-trek/.

16. Paul Andrews, "The Oldest Family Businesses in America," Family Business United, April 18, 2024, https://www.familybusinessunited.com/post/the-oldest-family-businesses-in-america.

17. "The American Family Today," Pew Research Center, December 17, 2015, https://www.pewresearch.org/social-trends/2015/12/17/1-the-american-family-today/.

18. John Piper, *Don't Waste Your Life* (Crossway, 2023), 46.

Chapter 3 Change Your Lens to a Generational View of Life

1. "How the Eyes Work," National Eye Institute, updated April 20, 2022, https://www.nei.nih.gov/learn-about-eye-health/healthy-vision/how-eyes-work.

2. "Complete Biblical Timeline," Bible Hub, accessed October 8, 2024, https://biblehub.com/timeline/. Psalm 78 is listed at 979 BC, and Nehemiah 7 is listed at 444 BC—535 years later.

3. Hugh Whelchel, "The Star of Bethlehem Points (Also) to the Eternal Impact of Our Work," Institute for Faith, Work & Economics, November 30, 2017, https://tifwe.org/the-star-of-bethlehem-work/.

4. "Complete Biblical Timeline," Bible Hub. Daniel came from the 550 BC period approximately, and the Magi arrived around AD 5—at least five hundred years later.

Chapter 4 Where Have We Gone Wrong?

1. Dennis T. Jaffe, *Borrowed from Your Grandchildren: The Evolution of 100-Year Family Enterprises* (Wiley, 2020), 36–37.

2. Bodie Hodge, "Ancient Patriarchs in Genesis," Answers in Genesis, January 20, 2009, https://answersingenesis.org/bible-characters/ancient-patriarchs-in-genesis/.

3. Sophia Kim, "The People Adam Met for 930 Years," Berit Theological Seminary and Graduate School, November 29, 2020, https://berit.us/true-peace-magazine/the-people-adam-met-for-930-years/.

4. Krishan Kumar, "Work and the Family," *Britannica*, August 29, 2024, https://www.britannica.com/topic/modernization/Work-and-the-family.

5. Kumar, "Work."

6. "Father Knows Best," IMDB, accessed November 19, 2024, https://www.imdb.com/title/tt0046600/?ref_=fn_al_tt_1.

7. "Leave It to Beaver," IMDB, accessed November 19, 2024, https://www.imdb.com/title/tt0050032/.

8. "My Three Sons," IMDB, accessed November 19, 2024, https://www.imdb.com/title/tt0053525/.

9. "The Waltons," IMDB, accessed November 19, 2024, https://www.imdb.com/title/tt0068149/.

10. "90's and 00's TV Series," IMDB, accessed November 19, 2024, https://www.imdb.com/list/ls096991576/.

11. "8 in 10 Americans Say Religion Is Losing Influence in Public Life," Pew Research Center, March 15, 2024, https://www.pewresearch.org/religion/2024/03/15/8-in-10-americans-say-religion-is-losing-influence-in-public-life/.

12. "In US, Decline of Christianity Continues at Rapid Pace," Pew Research Center, October 17, 2019, https://www.pewresearch.org/religion/2019/10/17/in-u-s-decline-of-christianity-continues-at-rapid-pace/.

13. "US Decline," Pew Research Center.

14. Mary Eberstadt, *How the West Really Lost God: A New Theory of Secularization* (Templeton Press, 2013), 20.

15. Jeremy Pryor, *Family Revision: How Ancient Wisdom Can Heal the Modern Family* (Family Teams, 2019), 5–10.

16. Pryor, *Family Revision*, 23.

17. Pryor, *Family Revision*, 16.

18. Preston Perry, *How to Tell the Truth: The Story of How God Saved Me to Win Hearts—Not Just Arguments* (Tyndale, 2024).

Chapter 5 Setting Your Course

1. James Hughes, *Family Wealth—Keeping It in the Family: How Family Members and Their Advisers Preserve Human, Intellectual, and Financial Assets for Generations* (Bloomberg, 2004).

2. Hughes, *Family Wealth*, 6.

3. Hughes, *Family Wealth*, 4.

4. Jaffe, *Borrowed*, 20.

5. Jaffe, *Borrowed*, 24.

6. Jaffe, *Borrowed*, 24.

7. Hughes, *Family Wealth*, 19.

8. Hughes, *Family Wealth*, 8–9.

9. "Florence Chadwick," Encyclopedia.com, accessed September 11, 2024, https://www.encyclopedia.com/people/sports-and-games/sports-biographies/florence-may-chadwick.

10. Ken Polk, *The Spirit of Wealth Preservation* (James E. Hughes Foundation, 2024), 35–45.

Chapter 6 Living by a Code of Conduct

1. "John Wooden," *Britannica*, accessed September 27, 2024, https://www.britannica.com/biography/John-Wooden.

2. Rick Reilly, "Coach John Wooden," Inspire21, January 28, 2010, https://inspire21.com/coachjohnwooden/.

3. "Coach Wooden's Answer to 'What's in Your Wallet?'—the Seven Point Creed," The John R. Wooden Course, November 25, 2020, https://www.thejohnrwoodencourse.com/coach-woodens-answer-to-whats-in-your-wallet-the-7-point-creed.

4. Katherine Eitel Belt, "The Code of the West," LionSpeak, accessed October 9, 2024, https://www.lionspeak.net/the-code-of-the-west/.

5. Jaffe, *Borrowed*, 38–39.

6. Jaffe, *Borrowed*, 38–39.

7. Larry Ballard, "Multigenerational Legacies—the Story of Jonathan Edwards," Youth With a Mission Family Ministries, July 1, 2017, https://ywam-fmi.org/news/multigenerational-legacies-the-story-of-jonathan-edwards/.

8. Ballard, "Multigenerational Legacies."

9. Jonathan Edwards, ed. Matt Perman, "The Resolutions of Jonathan Edwards," Desiring God, December 30, 2006, https://www.desiringgod.org/articles/the-resolutions-of-jonathan-edwards.

10. Christina Fox, "New Year's Resolutions: Aim for Godliness and God's Glory," The Gospel Coalition, January 2, 2015, https://www.thegospelcoalition.org/article/new-years-resolutions-and-jonathan-edwards/.

11. Ballard, "Multigenerational Legacies."

12. "How Many Israelites Really Left Egypt?," Jewish Belief Reimagined, accessed October 9, 2024, https://jewishbelief.com/how-many-israelites-left-egypt/.

Chapter 7 Repairing the Past

1. "The 25 Best Practices of Multi-Generational Families," Truist Wealth Center for Family Legacy, accessed October 14, 2024, https://

www.truist.com/resources/wealth/articles/the-25-best-practices-of-multi-generational-families.

2. Suzanna Andrews, "Shattered Dynasty," *Vanity Fair*, May 1, 2003, https://www.vanityfair.com/news/2003/05/andrews200305.

3. "Pritzker Family Settles Dispute with $900 Million Agreement," Philanthropy News Digest, January 12, 2005, https://philanthropynewsdigest.org/news/pritzker-family-settles-dispute-with-900-million-agreement.

4. Deniz Çam, "More Money, More Problems: Inside The Bitter Family Feuds of America's Richest Billionaire Clans," *Forbes*, December 17, 2020, https://www.forbes.com/sites/denizcam/2020/12/17/more-money-more-problems-inside-the-bitter-family-feuds-of-americas-richest-billionaire-clans/.

Chapter 8 Sharing Your Story

1. Jennifer Allen Craft, "Making a Place on Earth: Participation in Creation and Redemption Through Placemaking and the Arts" (PhD thesis, University of St. Andrews, 2013), 23.

2. "Complete Biblical Timeline," Bible Hub, accessed November 15, 2024, https://biblehub.com/timeline/.

3. Ira Glass, host, *This American Life*, podcast, episode 472, "Our Friend David," August 17, 2012, https://www.thisamericanlife.org/472/our-friend-david.

4. Mary Catherine Bateson, *Peripheral Visions: Learning Along the Way* (HarperCollins, 1994), 20.

5. Donald Miller, *A Million Miles in a Thousand Years: What I Learned While Editing My Life* (Thomas Nelson, 2009), 232.

6. "Storytelling and Cultural Traditions," *National Geographic*, accessed July 8, 2024, https://education.nationalgeographic.org/resource/storytelling-and-cultural-traditions/.

7. "Storytelling," *National Geographic*.

8. Hughes, *Family Wealth*, 12.

9. Maya Angelou, *I Know Why the Caged Bird Sings* (Random House, 1969).

10. Joshua 24:2: "Long ago your ancestors, including Terah the father of Abraham and Nahor, lived beyond the Euphrates River and worshiped other gods."

Chapter 9 Thriving Family Legacies of the Bible

1. "Bible Timeline," Bible Hub, accessed November 15, 2024, https://biblehub.com/timeline/. Second Kings 10 is listed at 841 BC and Jeremiah 35 at 588 BC.

2. "Bible Timeline: Old Testament," Bible Hub, accessed November 15, 2024, https://biblehub.com/timeline/old.htm.
3. "Jeremiah 35:19," Bible Hub, accessed October 14, 2024, https://biblehub.com/jeremiah/35-19.htm.
4. "Bible Timeline," Bible Hub.
5. "Bible Timeline," Bible Hub. Genesis 38 is listed at 1898 BC and Ruth at 1140 BC.
6. "Nahshon: An Emblem of Faithful Leadership in the Shadows of Biblical History," Digital Bible, November 9, 2023, https://digitalbible.ca/article-page/bible-study-biblical-characters-who-is-Nahshon-1699570180729x520539810699956800.
7. Christopher Eames, "Before Boaz and Ruth—Salmon and Rahab?," Armstrong Institute of Biblical Archaeology, July 29, 2021, https://armstronginstitute.org/359-before-boaz-and-ruth-salmon-and-rahab.
8. "Ruth 2: Pulpit Commentary," Bible Hub, accessed October 14, 2024, https://biblehub.com/commentaries/pulpit/ruth/2.htm.
9. "Ruth 2: Pulpit," Bible Hub. Genesis 38 is listed at 1898 BC and Nehemiah 11 at 444 BC.

Chapter 10 Legacy Families in History

1. Robert Balentine, "Avoiding the 'Shirtsleeves to Shirtsleeves' Phenomenon," Balentine, November 7, 2018, https://www.balentine.com/insights/shirtsleeves-to-shirtsleeves.
2. Natalie Rebehmed, "The Vanderbilts: How American Royalty Lost Their Crown Jewels," *Forbes*, updated June 17, 2019, https://www.forbes.com/sites/natalierobehmed/2014/07/14/the-vanderbilts-how-american-royalty-lost-their-crown-jewels/; Arthur T. Vanderbilt II, *Fortune's Children: The Fall of the House of Vanderbilt* (William Morrow, 1989).
3. Rebehmed, "The Vanderbilts."
4. Niall Ferguson, *The House of Rothschild—Money's Prophets, 1798–1842* (Penguin Books, 1998), 75.
5. Ferguson, *House of Rothschild*, 75.
6. Ferguson, *House of Rothschild*, 77.
7. Ferguson, *House of Rothschild*, 78.
8. Ferguson, *House of Rothschild*, 78 (italics added).
9. Ferguson, *House of Rothschild*, 79.
10. Ferguson, *House of Rothschild*, 79.
11. Ferguson, *House of Rothschild*, 79.
12. Ferguson, *House of Rothschild*, 7.
13. Ferguson, *House of Rothschild*, 7.
14. Ferguson, *House of Rothschild*, 8.

15. Jennifer Cook, "Rothschild Family: History, Net Worth and Facts," Investopedia, accessed May 9, 2024, https://www.investopedia.com/updates/history-rothschild-family/.

16. William T. O'Hara and Peter Mandel, "The World's Oldest Family Companies," Family Business, accessed October 14, 2024, https://www.griequity.com/resources/industryandissues/familybusiness/oldestinworld.html.

17. Herrera, "Building on Tradition."

18. Ferguson, *House of Rothschild*, 78.

19. Ferguson, *House of Rothschild*, 78.

20. "Five Failed Family Business Dynasties," Family Capital, September 10, 2015, https://www.famcap.com/2015/09/five-failed-family-business-dynasties/.

21. Robert Schoone-Jongen, "Flames in the Night: World War I Flares Up in Peoria, Iowa," *Origins Historical Magazine of the Archives* 36, no. 2 (2018): 4–6.

Chapter 11 A Legacy from Brokenness

1. Michael and Lauren McAfee, *Beyond Our Control: Let Go of Unmet Expectations, Overcome Anxiety, and Discover Intimacy with God* (Nelson Books, 2023).

2. Chris Fenner and Chuck Bumgardner, "It Is Well with My Soul with *Ville du Havre*," Hymnology Archive, updated July 15, 2021, https://www.hymnologyarchive.com/it-is-well-with-my-soul.

Chapter 12 Heaven in Sight

1. Nathan Knight, "How Often Do You Think About Heaven?," Desiring God, August 6, 2022, https://www.desiringgod.org/articles/how-often-do-you-think-about-heaven.

2. "622 Bible results for 'Heaven' from New International Version," Bible Gateway, accessed November 15, 2024, https://www.biblegateway.com/quicksearch/?quicksearch=heaven&version=NIV.

3. Jeffrey Kranz, "Who Wrote the Psalms? Hint: It Wasn't Just David," Overview Bible, October 12, 2018, https://overviewbible.com/who-wrote-psalms-besides-david/.

4. "Philippians," Insight for Living, 2010, https://insight.org/resources/bible/the-pauline-epistles/philippians.

About the Authors

DAVID GREEN borrowed $600 in 1970 to start making picture frames in a garage. He is now CEO of Hobby Lobby, which employs fifty thousand people at almost one thousand stores in forty-eight states and grosses $8 billion a year. The coauthor of *Leadership Not by the Book*, *The Leader's Devotional*, and *Giving It All Away . . . and Getting It All Back Again*, Green received the World Changer Award in 2013 and is a past recipient of the Ernst & Young Entrepreneur of the Year Award. David and his wife, Barbara, are the proud parents of three, grandparents of ten, and great-grandparents of seventeen (and counting). They live in Oklahoma City.

BILL HIGH is the CEO of Legacy Stone, a nonprofit ministry whose aim is to "raise family foundations for generational impact." The three themes for Bill's life are family, legacy, and generosity. After practicing law for twelve years, he moved into the charitable foundation world, where he began working with families. That work led to consulting work with families on crafting the plan for multigenerational legacies. He's worked with families in the United States and internationally. He's the author or coauthor of multiple books. He's married to his sweetheart, Brooke, and they have four children and four grandchildren. He can be found at BillHigh.com or LegacyStone.com.